Jack,

challenges are
opportunities in disguise.

Karl Vogt

MANAGE YOUR LIFE

Active Responses to Challenges

KENT VOIGT

LifeRich Publishing is a registered trademark of
The Reader's Digest Association, Inc.

LifeRich Publishing books may be ordered through booksellers or by contacting:

LifeRich Publishing
1663 Liberty Drive
Bloomington, IN 47403
www.liferichpublishing.com
1 (888) 238-8637

ISBN: 978-1-4897-1245-5 (sc)
ISBN: 978-1-4897-1244-8 (hc)
ISBN: 978-1-4897-1243-1 (e)

Library of Congress Control Number: 2017909409

Print information available on the last page.

LifeRich Publishing rev. date: 08/16/2017

CONTENTS

ACKNOWLEDGEMENTS

I want to acknowledge and thank my wife Terrie for the love and support she gave me as I sought to put on paper some of the lessons I've learned through years in education and ministry. As my trial reader, her reactions and ideas were invaluable. I also want to thank my daughters Tobi and Becky for their continuing encouragement.

Many thanks to my moral support team of Peter Hess, Ken Koroncey, Wally Dean, Leroy Phillips and Rick Ingolia. They demanded this book be written and weren't taking no for an answer.

Special thanks go to Elizabeth Sims, a superior writer and editor who took on the task of critiquing and shaping this manuscript in its earliest stages. Her experience, insight, frankness and encouragement contributed much to the final result. Special thanks as well go to Marj Scott for her invaluable input.

Last but certainly not least, I want to acknowledge and thank the many people who invited me into their lives, often at dark moments. They not only permitted me to work and learn with them but also inspired me with their courage, desire and determination to overcome life challenges.

INTRODUCTION

When you're up to your ears in trouble and fear, you don't want a book on philosophy or theology. You don't want a lecture. You want practical ideas you can use right now to settle the tempest. *Manage Your Life: Active Responses to Challenges* is such a resource.

The aim is to help readers understand and at least stabilize a troubling situation through positive practical action. It is not intended to be a substitute for professional care if needed.

Each chapter focuses on a single issue. Elements of a challenge are briefly explored then followed with recommended actions. Topics include finding love, working in stressful situations, helping without meddling, coping with illness, surviving political and economic wrangling, being the employee bosses want to keep and promote, dealing with anger, becoming prosperous and more. The topics are not all-inclusive nor need they be. Issues and techniques presented in one chapter may also apply to other concerns. Read through the book and extract ideas that make sense to you.

The book's content draws on my years of service in education and ministry. It includes lessons learned through personal challenges and from helping others work through frustrating and even frightening concerns. The examples are real and suggested actions based on experience.

It is my hope you find each chapter readable, interesting and most of all helpful. Life is not a smooth ride from start to finish. This is not necessarily bad. Ups and downs, while uncomfortable, foster personal growth and often lead to unimaginable good. May you find within these covers ideas that help you handle, keep or turn what comes your way into positive experiences.

CHAPTER 1

What Are You Thinking?

I trembled as the tiny car climbed slowly upward. I had decided it was time to get over my fear of heights so I went to Ohio's Cedar Point Amusement Park and boarded a car on their Magnum rollercoaster, then the highest in the world topping out at 210 feet.

As the car clanked its way upward my discomfort grew. At 200 feet my 12-year-old seatmate told me I had to put my hands over my head as the car moves over the top to begin its first downward plunge. "If you don't," he added, " you'll be a wimp." I looked straight ahead and ignored him. As we reached the top there was a moment when I could look out and see Canada over thirty miles away across Lake Erie. Yikes!

Wimpy didn't describe my feeling as our car glided over

the top of the first hill and began its sixty-mile per hour plunge toward the ground. Mercifully there was no time for panic. Hands over my head? Yeah right! I had a strangle hold on the bar across my lap. My body lifted off the seat then twisted sideways as we zoomed through turns. I admit I had a few unkind thoughts about the builder of this contraption. Fortunately, they were quickly replaced with the life affirming knowledge each plunge and turn was bringing me closer to the ground.

Minutes later my car arrived back at the boarding area. I caught my breath and realized I had done it! I had gone high enough to see across a world famous Great Lake and lived to tell about it. My fear of heights had momentarily been neutralized if not conquered. Many of my fellow ride passengers were squealing with delight causing me to understand the impact thoughts have on our experiences. Most people loved the ride. I didn't. We each got what we expected.

Still, I wondered how unanticipated events such as a car crash, act of war or crime affect our thoughts. There's no time to form a pre incident viewpoint in these situations. Things happen in microseconds. Yet, these terrible events often inspire human heroics, kindness and caring by nearby people. What were they thinking? I concluded our actions are not just reflex but directed by our thoughts about life – ours and others. I realized what we think matters.

Consider what happens when we have a bad day. The

MANAGE YOUR LIFE

MANAGE YOUR LIFE

alarm clock fails to wake us on time. We're late. We grab a coffee, jump in the car and head for the job. Are the other drivers really crazier than usual? Are office problems really tougher and take longer than those on a "normal" day? Did the coffee cup really cause us to spill its contents on our suit? Or, were we simply experiencing the result of our distracted, tired, hurried or negative thinking?

Now, consider a good day. Is success really easier to achieve? Is the day really brighter? Are people friendlier? Does time pass more quickly? What made the difference between our good and bad day? Thoughts. We can test this notion if we monitor our thoughts for a day and see what happens.

We can live with our thoughts and simply accept the results. Alternatively, we can keep those that serve us and challenge ones we feel to be unreasonable. The rollercoaster ride was my attempt to deal with an unreasonable fear of heights. I started the process by asking, "Will this ride put me in real danger? Knowing the care ride operators take to maintain their coasters, my answer was no. If the answer had been yes, then obviously taking the risk would have been foolhardy.

I decided my fear was exaggerated and the ride safe. So I hopped into the little car deciding to face my fear and minimize its impact on me in the future. I did it. I at least for the moment conquered a baseless limiting fear. I also

enhanced my self-image and prepared to tackle and eliminate other limiting thoughts.

Getting rid of an unreasonable fear is a starting point. If we want freedom from most limiting thoughts, we must also discard mental junk such as concern about past mistakes, misunderstandings, misdeeds and misbehaviors. We can do this through forgiveness. Forgiving others and ourselves cleans out useless thought burdens.

Follow forgiveness by learning to appreciate what it is to be human. We are imperfect creatures. We may have a raw fight or flee aspect but we can also learn to be kind, gentle and loving. We do this by focusing on good and desirable thoughts that minimize what separates and divides us from others.

While it's good to appreciate our worthiness, be careful. Should we slide into pride and ego, we can quickly turn positive thoughts negative. Many issue-oriented individuals learn this truth the hard way. Being right in our mind does not license us to force our ideas on others. When we adopt a point of view we must also be open to the thoughts of others. We live on a planet rife with diversity. Differences in race, color, creed, nationality, living styles and conditions are widespread. When we remain open to a variety of viewpoints, we permit valuable ideas and actions to enter our thinking.

The beliefs and attitudes we hold in thought direct our lives. We can dismiss guilt, anger, arrogance and other negative thoughts and have a good day. We can also dwell on them and invite misery.

The late Austrian psychiatrist and Holocaust survivor, Viktor Frankl, in his book "Man's Search for Meaning," observed many World War II Holocaust survivors owe their lives to their positive thoughts. He wrote:

> *"Life is not perfect. Despite good intentions and actions, misfortune can crash down on us. As challenging and difficult as these moments may be, they need not be devastating. Limit ill effects by seeking positive elements. Even in the darkest moments of illness, insurrection, accident and evil, good is present. The key to seeing them is to be looking for them. Everything can be taken from a man but one thing: the last of the human freedoms—to choose one's attitude in any given set of circumstances, to choose one's own way."*

When life does not go as we wish, it's time to ask, "What am I thinking? Are my thoughts filled with excitement and anticipation or fear, dread and uncertainty?" Establish a positive attitude and opportunities will appear out of nowhere. What are you thinking?

CHAPTER 2

Is It Time to Update Your Mental Processor?

A fresh from the factory computer is ready to accept and process whatever information and tasks we give it. It needs only power and instructions to become operational.

Like a new computer, a baby arrives ready to begin operating. It accepts instructions from parents, siblings and acquaintances. Over time more instructions and experiences are collected and filed away.

Eventually data stored on the computer and within the child becomes massive. Some data becomes outdated or corrupted. When this happens, thinking ability becomes sluggish or even unreliable. With a computer we run cleaning rebuilding software or replace the unit with a new one. Since we cannot replace a human with a new model, we must correct memory/processing issues.

We know we have a problem when our ability to recall or apply information correctly or quickly is reduced. Another problem sign occurs when we find our thoughts closed to new or different ideas.

Cleaning a human information processor begins with examining 'should' thoughts accumulated since birth. Should thoughts are mandates from parents, family members, school staff, religious leaders, governments, employers, politicians, the media, community organizations and even strangers. They may compliment other inputs but may also contradict them.

Clearing processing ability involves recognizing acquired information and instructions that no longer serve us. It may be outdated or proven false in the face of new data. Examples range from mildly amusing such as the old bromide, "You can't wear white after Labor Day," to hurtful and problematic thoughts about race, color, creed, ethnic origin, religion, nationality, age and so on.

My wife had this realization when struggling to show our five-year-old grandson how to do an operation on our home computer. An honors university graduate, a teacher, a leader in organizations and a computer user since the first PCs arrived, she still couldn't get her computer to do what she wanted. At that point our five-year-old grandson said politely, "Grandma can I show you how to do that?" He took control of the keyboard and mouse and promptly completed the task. His memory was not overloaded with should ideas. He drew instead on intuitive ability and the task was done.

I remember this story every time I struggle with my computer. I can't help but wonder if the problem is the computer or me? I usually find the answer when I open my thinking enough to consult a manual. Situations like these led me to develop a five-step approach to clearing and rejuvenating my thinking. So far it seems to work:

- **Step One:** Let go of as much fear and anxiety as possible by taking a few minutes to relax. Sit comfortably and breathe easily while you moderately tighten as many of the voluntary muscles in your body as you feel you can. Next, starting with your scalp, release the tightened muscles by group moving from the top of your head to the bottom of your feet. As you become comfortable you'll notice a calm descending upon you. Once calmness is achieved, move to step two.

- **Step Two:** In your relaxed state, think about issues bothering you. Acknowledge that even though they seem big at the moment they are really just a small part of your life and the Universe.

- **Step Three:** Consider whether your concerns are real or the result of uncertainty and fear based on an excess of stored 'should' thoughts. If you're unsure, seek additional information on-line, in books, articles or from others you consider knowledgeable.

- **Step Four:** Remind yourself life is ever changing. Change brings uncertainty. Decide you will not make matters worse by simply accepting the ideas of others. Recognize you are free to set your own life path. Let go of pressure from others.

- **Step Five:** Commit to an open mind. Examine your ideas and those of others in light of changing circumstances. Use your experiences and knowledge in the process but be open to change, if and when it makes sense to you.

CHAPTER 3

The Unexpected May Be a Gift

Eighteenth century writer, Horace Walpole, coined the word serendipity to describe a phenomenon he first came across while reading an ancient Persian fairy tale.

The tale relates the experiences of three princes from the mythical kingdom of Serendip. They decide to leave home and roam the world in search of treasure. Despite little success finding treasure, they do find things they come to realize are far more valuable.

Returning home, they decide life is filled with wonderful tricks intended to help us acquire what we need rather than what we seek. The key to activating this option is to allow it to happen. The story behind the discovery of the world's first antibiotic, penicillin, is an example.

In 1928 Scottish physician Alexander Fleming was

studying the bacteria that frequently infects wounds. People with repairable wounds were dying from infection more often than the wounds themselves. He determined to do something about it. Tasking himself to find a substance that would kill the bacteria without harming the patient, he conducted numerous experiments with no success.

Frustrated, he noticed a pesky mold growing on some lab dishes waiting to be washed. Looking carefully at them he also noticed any bacteria that came near the mold quickly died. Based on this observation he began experimenting with the mold. Every time he introduced bacteria to it, the mold eliminated it.

Experiments revealed the mold had no negative effect on larger organisms. It was then he realized he had, by chance, found what he was looking for. He called the mold penicillin and made it available to others. Millions of people since 1928 owe their lives to Dr. Fleming's serendipitous discovery.

Closer to home, I had my own serendipitous experience. I turned thirteen in 1955 and planned to celebrate with a week at summer Boy Scout camp. All campers were required to get a pre-camp physical exam. I went to the family physician and promptly failed the exam.

The doctor discovered the main artery between my heart and legs was constricted. This apparent birth defect permitted adequate blood flow to support a toddler and young boy's body but barely enough for a teen and nowhere near enough for a full-grown man. Untreated, the doctor said, it would take my life possibly within five years.

Searching for a cure he read a medical journal article discussing an experimental surgical procedure for my condition. Invented at Johns Hopkins Hospital in Baltimore, Md., the procedure was in trials. He made a few phone calls and promptly learned one of the trial sites was scheduled that summer at Henry Ford Hospital in Detroit. He sent my parents and me to Ford where we met the doctors involved. I was accepted into the program.

The surgery was successfully completed that July. Since it was a new procedure, there was no indication as to the long-term effect of the fix. To be safe, the doctors decided I was to follow a sedentary six-week recovery period and avoid strenuous physical activity for the next ten years with check-ups at regular intervals. My dream of a sports career ended that August. But I was alive!

To keep me immobile but mentally busy during my six-week recovery, my parents gave me a small shortwave radio kit to build. I made it, turned it on and the world of international broadcasting and radio technology caught my interest. That radio sparked what was to be a lifelong interest in broadcasting and electronics.

My last post surgical physical exam was conducted just after my twenty-third birthday. The doctors then concluded the surgery was a total success. Most physical restrictions were lifted. I could again be active. By that time however, my interest in radio and electronics had supplanted more active alternatives.

I earned amateur radio and commercial broadcast engineer licenses during my restricted years. I worked at my high school radio station leading to a job at a local commercial radio station. I earned a college degree and took a teaching job. I was at the beginning of what came to be a thirty-four year career path that also included jobs in school management and finally work as a university professor. My specialty was the use of communication technologies in teaching and learning. The unexpected discovery and repair of a birth defect not only saved my life but led me to successful and rewarding careers.

My story is not unique. Billions of people suffer what appears to be a loss only to discover it was the key to a far greater good. The princes of Serendip were right. If we permit it, life wants to bring us wonders beyond our imagination.

Benefitting from life's serendipitous twists requires a willingness to flow with rather than battle the unexpected. If you're interested, here are suggestions on getting started:

- **Get into or stay in action**. Had I simply sat on that back porch feeling sorry for myself, the good I later experienced might never have happened. Serendipity rewards those who look for possibilities. Noted theoretical physicist and cosmologist, Stephen Hawking, lost the use of his body through ALS (Lou

Gehrig's Disease). His mind was not affected. Rather than waste away, he turned his efforts to what he could do - think. He theorized and with help published volumes on natural phenomena. In so doing, he changed ideas about our world and the universe.

- **Don't expect something for nothing.** Give of your time and talents and be flexible. At thirteen I never saw myself as a teacher or technology expert. Staying in motion led me to unimaginable good including my wonderful wife and family and later ministry and chaplaincy.

- **Stick with an objective.** Don't stop when you feel resistance. Resistance merely means you're moving forward. A boat must push water away from its bow to make progress. See yourself doing the same with life.

CHAPTER 4

Make Your Job Work for You

It was a dream job for a seventeen year-old. I was to be a "board man" at a commercial radio station. In 1959 recorded music was replacing live radio drama and music programs. Rock and roll music was emerging and radio disc jockeys began playing recorded versions of the songs from remote locations such as car dealerships and fast food restaurants. Specially built trailer studios emblazoned with radio station call letters and large picture windows that permitted people to see the disc jockey at work appeared all around major cities. I was going to be part of this. My job at station headquarters would be to support disc jockeys at remote sites. I would control sound levels, play commercials, insert local and network newscasts and anything else the disk jockey needed.

I got the job when the local radio station manager contacted my high school looking for a student interested in a part time after school job. Three years of technical and on air experience with the school's low power FM radio station and the recommendation of the station's sponsoring teacher got me the job.

The first time I pressed the switch to start a broadcast at the commercial station I was in a state of semi-controlled terror. I was sending programs to thousands of listeners in the Detroit area. Settling my nerves was the thought I was also getting paid to listen to top 40 music and do work I loved. I was so lucky.

Over the years I've come to realize I was far luckier than I knew at the time. In addition to a profitable part-time job, I learned about working in the "real world".

My disk jockey partner helped make the job fun. He was professional yet zany. His humor included occasional pranks on me "to keep you awake," he'd say. Other staff members, older broadcast pros, were not thrilled at having a 'kid' invade their workplace. Taking the hazing without complaint attracted the attention of three of the station's more experienced staff. They decided to take me on as a project. One taught me announcing, another music programming, and the third focused on how to work with others and become a valued employee. These instructions have stayed with me throughout my life and have been crucial to my success in every job I've ever had.

Dave, an announcer/newsman with a velvet voice and skills that attract listeners in numbers, taught me announcing. Reading commercials and news out loud with emphasis and expression is more difficult than most people think. My first lesson was to say the station's call letters correctly. They started with the letter W which Dave emphasized is pronounced double u not dubbya as was common at the time. He took me through a variety of often mispronounced or misspoken words. I learned milk is spoken with an emphasis on the short i sound – it's milk not melk. The word hot should be spoken fast and hard whereas cold needs to be uttered slowly and lightly (coooold). I learned to handle fast paced on-air conditions and cover glitches with commentary. Dave was my idol. His instructions have been a tremendous help in public speaking required by my later education and ministry work.

Jack, a former Hollywood song and dance man, knew the music of every genre. He taught me to match music to the time of day, season of the year and nature of the audience (men/women). Among his tricks was playing a popular Christmas tune or two on a hot summer day or a beach tune at Christmas time. "They spice things up and guarantee listener phone calls," he said. Jack loved his work and was often seen dancing to the music next to the control console.

Charlie, the program director, was experienced in all phases of the business. He took me on with the objective of making me the kind of employee bosses and colleagues like. According to his philosophy a job, no matter what it involves, is an opportunity. "When you appreciate that fact," he'd say, "you're on the way to being a winner." Charlie had eight dos and don'ts that he said apply to any job I might have. His list was and remains priceless. I've lived by them for over fifty years, shared them with my children and with each new employee who ever worked with me. Here's what Charlie's said.

- **Rule One**: Keep your eyes and ears open. Be aware of what's happening around you. Listen to and observe your coworkers. You'll learn who is happy, who is not, who is working hard and who is hardly working. You'll learn about office relationships and politics and get a sense of how well the business is doing. Best of all, you will be aware of future opportunities and know how to prepare for them.

- **Rule Two**: Keep your mouth closed! Never gossip. People who start or spread gossip are listened to but seldom liked or trusted. They frequently find themselves passed over for promotions or among the first to be let go in difficult times. Be friendly and smile often. It's a sign of acceptance. Keep office conversations light and focused on the job. Social media had not been invented when Charlie shared his wisdom. Had it been around, I'm certain he would have cautioned against discussing the job on it. He felt what happens at the office should stay at the office. Once something is said publicly, it's out there forever and can come back to haunt.

- **Rule Three**: Never forget everyone's first priority is them. "Jobs mean security," he'd say. "As new positions arise you'll probably find yourself in competition for them with one or more of your colleagues. People you expect to support you may fade under pressure from others. Some may even try to undermine you. Nice people can be vicious when it comes to their livelihood. When you seek advancement you're usually on your own."

- **Rule Four:** Never forget the one who pays you has the right to decide what you do. The boss is giving you money to provide a service to the company and to him. Give him what he wants then surprise him by doing a little more. This action marks you as a dedicated employee. If you see a better way to do a task, privately and diplomatically suggest it to your boss (your immediate boss please! Don't ever go over his or her head to a higher-level boss…deadly!). Get approval before acting on your ideas. Be prepared for a refusal. If that happens, do as originally requested. If you feel you cannot do something you're asked to do or that the request is illegal or immoral, get another job.

- **Rule Five:** Charlie was a strong respecter of company property. He emphasized it is never OK to take company property or use its facilities, tools or supplies for personal projects without first obtaining permission. This rule applies even to pencils, paper, use of copiers, etc. Establish a reputation that you are 100% trustworthy and respectful of company property.

- **Rule Six:** When it comes to talking about your company, Charlie advised avoiding negative comments. He said this advice also applies to thoughts about your boss and other employees. He quoted an old expression that says, "When you speak ill of your job and the people you work with, you speak ill of yourself." After all, if things are so bad, why are you working there?

- **Rule Seven:** Never leave a job with bad feelings or speak ill of a former employer. Past work relationships have a way of coming back to haunt or help with future employment. Keep your words positive and your opinions to yourself. Keep your work experiences and personal happenings private. In this Facebook, Twitter, Linked In, email era it's easy to tell friends about your work. Think before you do so. Better... don't. Yes, you read this earlier. I just wanted to emphasize the point. These sites are not as secure as you might like to believe.

- **Rule Eight:** Keep everything you do through work phones and mail (emails & Internet connections didn't exist then) business related. Courts have repeatedly ruled business systems and the things done on or through them belong to the business. Many employers monitor employee emails, phone calls and Internet searches. Don't do or say anything through these tools that you don't want your boss, colleagues or the world to know.

Most of us will put in thirty or more years working at income earning jobs. How we go about them has a tremendous impact on our life quality. Whether we're a boss or an employee, it's important to strive to be the best we can be not only with our tasks but in relations with other people. Seeing each position as an important stepping-stone to the next prepares us for continuing success. Always think before you speak or act. Walk the kinder gentler path. It's smoother and almost always more productive.

CHAPTER 5

How To Complain So Others Will Listen

I noticed cracking on the sidewalls of tires I'd purchased five months earlier. A trip back to the national brand tire store where I bought them ended in frustration. The manager acknowledged the problem and offered to replace the tires under warranty. He then added, "You'll have to pay a pro-rated amount for the miles you've driven on them." The tires were warranted for 45,000 miles. I had driven them less than ten percent of that amount. Paying even a small amount for their poor performance seemed inappropriate. I objected. The store manager sympathized but said the fee was company policy and he couldn't override it. I didn't argue. I paid the fee then took my concern to the company's national customer relations office through a letter.

Using humor to get attention, I told them I was unhappy

with their company's fee for partial use warranty policy. I then told a little melodramatic story.

I said my father always bought their tires and told me as I grew up I could depend on their brand. Naturally, when I needed new tires I bought their product. I mentioned how sad I was when the tires did not live up to their claims and my expectations. Making matters worse, I said, was the demand I pay a fee for replacements. I explained I felt the charge to be inappropriate thus I was bringing my concern to the attention of the national office. "I'm certain," I added, "you must not be aware how this policy affects loyal customers. After all, my Dad always said yours is a great company that stands behind its products and cares for its customers."

A few weeks later I received a reply signed by the vice president for customer relations. He said my letter had been circulated throughout the office. He noted it was rare for a customer to use story humor rather than anger to bring a problem to their attention. He also said my point was well made and the company was looking at changing their warranty use fee policy.

The VP's letter included a check reimbursing the amount I was charged for replacement tires and a voucher toward the purchase of new tires the next time I needed them. He thanked me for my patience and for bringing the warranty shortcoming to his attention. My problem was resolved and all parties seemed to feel good about it.

Humor doesn't work in every situation but why start a

conversation with accusations, anger and hostility? No one likes to be yelled at. A complaint expressed pleasantly is more likely to achieve a positive result.

It is best to simply and directly state the issue up front then follow up with what you feel would be a satisfactory solution. Be reasonable. Assume the company is honorable. Never make accusations.

When my youngest daughter graduated from high school. We held a backyard party to celebrate. In addition to soft drinks, we had a small supply of beer for adults. A guest called me over and showed me a sealed beer can that had been barely filled at the factory. It was an obvious defect and no big deal. Later, in a whimsical mood, I decided to tell the brewery about it.

I wrote my typical humor letter saying when I finally sat down to sip a cold beer after the party I found the only one left was a sealed nearly empty can. I said I missed enjoying their fine product and suggested they check their quality control system. I mailed the letter and forgot about it.

A few weeks later I received a letter containing a very terse response from a company representative who indirectly suggested I was not being truthful. Her letter included the line, "Since you didn't keep the can there is nothing we can do for you." That response irked me. I did have the offending can so I packaged it up with another letter beginning with the words: "Ah Ha!" I told her I did keep the can and was enclosing it so she and her quality control staff could inspect it. I asked nothing of the company. I then sent the package and again forgot about it.

A week later, my wife called me at work saying, "Well, you've really done it this time!" It seems a semi-trailer beer truck with the company logo plastered all over it pulled in front of our house. The driver got out and hand delivered a case of the company's beer. My wife laughingly said, "Our neighbors are going to think we're such heavy drinkers we require beer home delivered by semi." I never received a letter of explanation but clearly my letter prompted a positive response.

I'm seldom ignored or mistreated when I handle a problem with humor. However, never ever be sarcastic! Sarcasm is hostile and will almost guarantee a negative response. There's a life principle that suggests we get what we give. Store clerks, customer service representatives and others charged with handling product or service problems are people. They have feelings and emotions. Honor this fact by treating them well and you'll almost always receive kindness in return.

Both of our daughters worked in the retail industry when they were fresh out of high school. They each tell stories of people arriving at the store pre-mad and ready to fight. This situation became more frequent when they went into management. It bothered them until they internalized the idea a person yelling at them was really yelling at the store. They adopted the idea a yeller was talking to their store shirt, not them personally. Both noted it is hard to help someone who is angry. When someone yells at a person who can resolve a problem, they destroy that person's incentive to be helpful.

Effective complaining is common sense not a special talent. Here are time-tested techniques to consider:

- Let go of anger, frustration and hurt feelings. They're useless when you're trying to get positive action on a problem. See the person who will receive your complaint as an individual not an anonymous company figure. They may be wearing a company shirt but they are not the company.

- State your problem clearly, briefly and politely. Tell the business official what you would like done. Be reasonable. Be friendly and if it suits the situation use humor- but never sarcasm.

- If you meet with rejection, calmly ask why and what you can do to alter the decision. If necessary, acknowledge the person you're speaking to may not be in a position to alter company policy. Ask if there is someone else who might have that authority. Keep your tone friendly.

- Never threaten to tell everyone you know or area newspapers and TV stations how terribly you've been treated. Don't threaten to complain to your state's attorney general or sue. Companies know you're unlikely to do these things especially over items valued under several hundred dollars. Saying such things just reduces your credibility.

- If your problem is not resolved locally, write a letter to the company's customer service department containing the details of your problem. Request help at the corporate level.

- Unless the monetary loss is great, forget legal action. Legal remedies can take years to resolve and, if you lose, can be costly. A better alternative is to simply write off the loss, stop doing business with the company and put the problem out of your mind.

CHAPTER 6

Want to be Prosperous?

"All you need in this life is ignorance and confidence; then success is sure." With these words American writer Mark Twain (Samuel Clemens) summed up a success formula that has worked for millions of people. Twain wasn't promoting lack of education or arrogance. He was pointing out the characteristics of winners. Twain's idea of ignorance was the ability to believe in something even when others say it's impossible. By confidence he meant seeing oneself successful despite other's failure.

Apple co-founder Steve Jobs, media star Oprah Winfrey, Motown's Barry Gordy Jr., TV host Ellen DeGeneres and many others didn't know they lacked the knowledge or resources to be successful. They unknowingly adopted Twain's recipe for success. They took an idea, added a heaping helping of belief in its possibility, mixed in purposeful action and their dreams materialized. Along the way they added a healthy dose of willingness to keep working when challenges made success seem unlikely. Each became a leader in their chosen field.

Movie director, producer and screenwriter Steven Spielberg followed the same prescription. Now considered one of the founding pioneers of the new Hollywood era, he struggled to get into the business. His applications for admission to the prestigious University of Southern California School of Cinematic Arts were rejected multiple times. Left on his own, he took his belief that he was a movie producer/director to heart and made low budget movies on simple equipment. His work was so good his productions eventually drew the attention of people in the industry and to his first blockbuster film, "Jaws," in 1975. Its success led Hollywood studios to open their doors to him. He since created three Academy Award winning films, four primetime TV Emmy Award winning programs and seven daytime Emmy Award winning shows. Added together, his projects have grossed more than $9 billion. Spielberg is a poster child for Twain's "ignorance and confidence" notion.

Success requires belief and effort as much or more than talent. Thankfulness is also helpful. Being thankful for ideas, opportunities and even failures primes our mental prosperity pump. It opens our thinking to otherwise overlooked or discarded ideas and options that might benefit us.

I became aware of priming as a twelve year old Boy Scout on an overnight camping trip. The camp had sleeping cabins but lacked indoor plumbing. Water for cooking and washing had to be brought in a bucket at a time from an outside well. When I was assigned to the task, I discovered it wasn't as easy as it sounded. The well had a hand-operated pump. I knew what I wanted, put forth the effort to get it and believed I would be successful but nothing happened. No matter how hard I moved the handle up and down water would not flow out of the spigot. A more experienced camper saw me struggling and calmly asked if I'd primed the pump. "Primed?" I answered, "What is primed?" He explained hand pumps need a small amount of water poured into the top of the mechanism before moving the handle. I learned the water creates a vacuum seal that permits the pump to suck water up out of the ground and into my bucket. I did as told and soon had a bucket full of water. Lesson learned. When you want something, be prepared to "prime the pump" by doing something that will get things running. Spielberg went out and made a low budget movie rather than just keep knocking on doors closed to him.

An idea you think is doable, belief you can do it and willingness to do the tasks needed to prime the process and get the job done are key factors to prosperity. There is still another. Be open to surprises. Be willing to take side trips down alternate paths. They don't always appear but when they do the result can be amazing.

The late Dr. John Kellogg created corn flakes as a health food in the late 1800's. Intended for patients with special dietary needs at his Kalamazoo, Michigan sanitarium, they were so tasty and easy to prepare people leaving the sanitarium clamored for boxes to take home. When they introduced corn flakes to friends, grocers were besieged with requests to carry them. The demand became so great Kellogg's brother built a factory to make them and, as they say, the rest is history. Corn flakes and other dried cereals now comprise a multibillion-dollar business. The sanitarium is closed but the Kellogg name continues.

Another surprise was the microwave oven. It came as a side effect during the development of aircraft detecting radar systems. The story is an engineer developing this early warning equipment noticed while he was scanning the skies for airplanes, chocolate bars in his shirt pocket were melting. He realized the microwaves used in radar were the cause. Before long his discovery led to a new kitchen-cooking appliance called the "radar" range. The microwave oven as it is known today, has since become one of the most used kitchen appliances in the world.

Other unexpected marvels include Velcro, x-rays, Teflon, stainless steel, plastic, superglue, potato chips, chocolate chip cookies, ice cream cones, matches, bubble wrap, Post-it-Notes, Silly Putty, Kleenex and Coca Cola. Look them up on the Internet. The stories behind each are fascinating.

If prosperity is the goal, we can enhance our chances by remembering ignorance, confidence, action and openness to surprise. Oh yes, and don't forget to prime the pump by being thankful for opportunities.

CHAPTER 7

There's No Time Like the Present

"You need to take better care of yourself," my doctor said. He'd been telling me this for years but today there seemed urgency in his tone. "Your tests suggest a few things need attention. Fortunately with lifestyle changes you can get them under control." I knew he was right. I also knew the task would be a challenge for me.

Like many people, I find it difficult to do what's in my best interest if it means not doing things I've grown to enjoy like eating sweets and avoiding exercise. When I see trim athletic people I wonder if they know something I don't. A friend answered my question.

He and I went through high school together and were both underweight at graduation. Over the years I added excess pounds. He weighs a bit more than high school but is still quite trim. I asked how he stays this way. "I learned the value of moment-by-moment thinking," he said.

He explained we are born with powerful thinking capabilities. We use them to make sense of our world and set our course of action. While thoughts are clearly important, they don't by themselves make things happen. We can only create, alter and make preparations for the future in the present. Only what we do each day impacts what happens to us tomorrow. "If you want health tomorrow," he said, "you have to do something about it today, now, in the present."

He once worked in the weight management industry where he said he saw the effects of this principle close up. "People often decide they no longer want to be overweight and picture themselves thin in the future. Each day however they sabotage their desire by continuing habits that made them overweight. "They think thin but eat thick," he added. When they fail to achieve their expected goal they give up believing it can't be done. "I stay trim," he said, "because I discovered the magic is in the present. Do what needs doing today and achieving what you want tomorrow is all but assured.

Another friend is a master at using the present. He rarely lets a day go by without achieving something he wants. He does it with a to do list. As he adds items, he gives each a priority rating of A, B, C or D with A as most pressing and D the least. He also adds due dates. When he gets up each morning he takes out his to do list, adds, deletes or adjusts items then makes a short list for the day. He puts the most difficult or challenging task at the top of the list to be tackled first. When I asked why, he said, "If I do the toughest job first, everything after it seems easy." He says it's a mental trick that motivates him to get in action rather dreading and procrastinating.

Following my doctor's advice means doing something today not just thinking about it. A healthy body requires health-building activities every day. Gaining wealth requires establishing a plan and working at it every day. If we want joy, love and happiness, do what's required to get them.

There is no time like the present. It is the only time we can achieve anything. The magic behind it is action - today, this minute, this second. Staying in the present is helped by regularly asking, "Is what I'm doing at this moment taking me closer to my desires or keeping me away from them?" We get what we give and we can only give in the present.

CHAPTER 8

Are You Helping or Meddling?

When I was twelve, my Boy Scout troop was scheduled to participate in an outdoor winter skills program. Boys were divided into teams and each team was to make an Alaska style dog sled to carry gear over the snow to various skill stations. One scout would be the driver in back while the others pulled the sled.

My father offered to help build our team sled. Getting boys together often enough to get the job done became difficult so my team left the job to my dad and me to finish. I was to be the prime builder and my dad the helper. I knew from the outset this could be a problem.

My father was the most honest and trustworthy man I've ever known. A lawyer and judge, he was unbiased and frowned on courtroom theatrics. He kept cases focused on facts not fantasy.

He had another characteristic however that was occasionally difficult for me to handle. Incredibly talented at everything he did, he was also something of a perfectionist. This factor made building the Boy Scout sled an ordeal for me.

My father would frequently step in to help me with a task to make sure it was done right. Before long, my role as sled builder evolved into holding, sanding and watching. I eventually stopped working and let him finish the project. The completed sled was beautiful but it wasn't my sled. I didn't get to build it. I knew he was just trying to be helpful but he unintentionally took away my pride and sense of accomplishment.

Most people want to be helpful and this is, of course, good. But there is also such a thing as being too helpful. Taking over a task, helping without being asked or giving advice (aka criticizing) no matter the intention is not helping. It is meddling and meddling seldom turns out well.

We all want to feel good about ourselves. We don't want our errors, misjudgments, ineptitudes, bumps and bruises known let alone highlighted by a would-be helper. This human characteristic makes helping tricky. Offer it when not requested and a would-be helper may be viewed as disrespectful.

When observing someone who seems befuddled or in a mess, it's usually best to leave them alone unless they request help or you see the situation is potentially dangerous. If however you see an easy fix and just can't stand watching someone struggle you might risk a mild intervention by first asking if they would like a hand. If they say no, walk away.

In my golfing days, I used to have a terrible slice driving off a tee. One sunny Saturday I decided to try to correct the problem at a local driving range. After hitting half a bucket of balls with disastrous results, a young woman dressed in University of Michigan woman's golf team sweats came up and very politely asked if she could make a suggestion. I immediately said yes. She showed me I was holding the club improperly. She demonstrated then had me try it. I did as suggested and the first ball I hit went 250 yards right down the middle of the fairway. Two more did the same. I thanked her profusely. She smiled and said your welcome adding, "You were driving me crazy with that swing. I just had to say something."

The young woman wisely asked if she could help before acting. A question does not assume someone can't handle things. It's merely an offer of assistance. You'll likely get a yes or no.

If invited to help, start with a brief conversation. This helps both of you determine if you're receptive to one another. No one wants to feel they've lost control of their lives. Conversation gives the person time to consider if they really want your assistance.

I deal regularly with people struggling with medical

problems. If their need is physical, I leave them to medical staff.

My role as a chaplain is with thoughts and feelings. Before I enter a hospital room, I knock. This simple act avoids startling a patient, shows respect and gives them a moment to prepare for a visitor. If invited in, I introduce myself and immediately tell them the purpose of my visit is simply to find out how they're doing and if they need anything.

If they seem responsive, I ask a few non-invasive questions. This permits them to tell me if they feel like talking and puts them in control of the conversation. Based on their input I may move on using a technique called purposeful listening.

I ask if they mind telling me why they came to be hospitalized. This question again puts them in control and starts information sharing. I respond occasionally to reassure them I'm listening. Sidelined in a hospital bed can make a person feel lonely and isolated. Even with staff doing things to and for them day and night they may still feel physically and emotionally vulnerable. I try to fill that void at least for a few minutes.

If it seems appropriate, I ask if they're concerned about anything in particular. You might think their main concern would center on their physical condition. This is not always the case. I once asked this of a woman who immediately blurted out, "Who's going to care for my children?" It turned out her doctor told her she would need several days of hospitalization. Had I focused only on her physical situation, I might have missed this important issue. She gave me the names and numbers of relatives and friends who she hoped would help but who she hesitated to ask. I did the asking and the issue was quickly resolved.

Lesson learned. When you want to help someone, don't assume you know what help is most important to them. Ask before acting. It almost always yields better results.

Another patient was agitated. Staff asked me to see if I could calm him down. He jumped at the chance to share his thoughts. He was worried if the diagnosis was correct, the treatment adequate and about his long-term prospects. When he stopped talking, I asked if he had discussed the diagnosis with his doctor. He said yes. I asked if he had a problem with it. He said no, telling me he is just a worrier. I asked if he knew what treatment was to be used. He said he did and he was satisfied it was correct.

I asked him to help me understand his illness by telling me what he would advise me to do if I had the same problem. The question took him away from being the object of help to being a helper. A few moments passed then he looked at me and spoke about his illness.

He then told me (and himself) he was going to be OK and what he needed to do to stay that way. He was able to internalize his doctor's comments by making the health advice his own.

Purposeful listening is helping without appearing to

tell others how to live. Purposeful listening acknowledges people are independent beings worthy of respect. It guides conversation until the person needing help is able to resolve a problem to their satisfaction.

That said, I must add there is an exception to this approach. If a situation involves a potential life and death emergency (an automobile accident for example), it is OK to step in and give immediate direct assistance without asking *if you are qualified to do so and your actions will not add to the problem or place you or others in jeopardy.*

A desire to help is admirable. It can enhance the lives of all involved. But, before doing so, be certain your help is needed and desired. Wherever possible, wait to be invited before moving ahead.

CHAPTER 9

Look for the Upside in Down Moments

I was speechless when she walked in the door. Her father asked to bring his daughter along to help him conduct a staff work session at the school district where I was the media director. I expected a twelve year old. Instead the girl at his side was a beautiful twenty-three year old woman. Her father introduced us adding she had recently graduated from college and signed a contract to teach in my district. Before leaving that day we had a date for dinner. We began seeing each other regularly and a year later, were married. The story behind this wonderful outcome is an example of how a series of down experiences can lead to very up moments.

Terrie was an honors student at Michigan State University and very active in campus happenings including a sought after sorority. Before graduation she had visions of a teaching career in an exciting east coast city.

Asked to be a bridesmaid in a sorority sister's wedding in Boston, she jumped at the opportunity. Boston was the quaint New England historic atmosphere she had dreamed about. While there, she applied for teaching jobs in several east coast communities. It didn't take long for rejection letters to arrive. One of them made it clear east coast school districts, at least at that time, gave priority to east coast university graduates. Employment for a Midwesterner was at best only a slim possibility. She reluctantly turned her attention to Michigan where her personality and academic record quickly landed her a job in my school district. She later told me the day she signed the contract was a low moment. It meant her dream of east coast living was, at best on hold.

A few years older than Terrie, I had dated wonderful women but never found the 'one.' I had pretty much concluded bachelorhood was my lot. Then Terrie entered my life. Bright, fascinating and filled with intoxicating joy I couldn't believe my good fortune. She was everything I'd been looking for and more. Several months of dating confirmed she was the one for me. She seemed to share my feelings. When I asked her to marry me she said yes. I'm happy to report we've been a joyful combination for almost fifty years. Making things better, we have two wonderful daughters and two delightful grandchildren who bring light and love into our lives.

Mulling over the events that brought us together I

recognize an example of life's wonderful irony. With me reluctantly and sadly deciding my destiny was bachelorhood and Terrie anticipating a dull Midwest future, our thoughts were well down on our emotion scales. But, a valuable lesson was in process.

Things that seem bleak may actually be signaling something exciting is coming our way. Finding my fabulous wife is at the top of my list but I now realize I've had many other wonderful happenings come this way. An upside almost always follows a down time if we remain open enough to see and grab it.

War, natural disasters and personal crises are certainly down times and difficult to endure. Still by limiting our emotional responses to them and keeping active, we can often find opportunities to bring something positive into our lives.

Apple Computer co-founder, Steve Jobs, was once booted out of Apple by its board of directors. His creative yet aggressive and abrasive style was thought to be detrimental to internal and external business relationships. The Apple board decided the company needed a more polished business oriented individual versed in "proper" corporate behavior at the company helm. This was clearly not a good time for Jobs.

No longer tied to Apple's corporate bureaucracy and with a healthy payout, Jobs realized he was free to indulge his creative notions. He founded a company he called NEXT. Here he and a few of his visionary colleagues were free to explore cutting edge technology and create innovative products unencumbered by corporate bureaucracy.

A period of poor economic performance at Apple coincided with Jobs phenomenal rise with NEXT. Apple board members recognizing the importance of an innovative spirit to their company's future took hat in hand and re-recruited Jobs.

Job's free wheeling spirit, now acknowledged and appreciated at Apple's top corporate levels, led to the company's resurgence. Legendary new products like the iPod, iPhone, and more flew out of research and development offices. Jobs changed the company and in the process the computer industry, the music industry, the communications industry and office processes. Jobs may have been at a low point when ousted but that down experience by both he and Apple enabled each to recognize what was needed to move forward. Once back together the sky became the limit. Jobs became more business like and the company more willing to innovate.

Whether something is bad or not is a decision not an unchangeable reality. It is a signal we need to pause and look around before moving on. There are opportunities in everything and this is especially true when we think something is bad. These are the moments when looking for the upside of down is advised.

One word impedes progress toward good however. It is the word should. Thinking should destroys creativity.

It suggests there is a right and wrong way to do things. It practically guarantees missing good trying to reach us.

Life prefers balance. When a problem appears, a solution is usually not far behind. This is the upside of down. If we will but pause before labeling something good or bad, our lives can be greatly enhanced. The good may not come as we expect but if we keep our minds open, we will recognize it none-the-less.

CHAPTER 10

How to Find Love

My uncle was a tall handsome man who enhanced his stature with a ready smile and firm handshake. My father's brother, a lawyer, wounded World War II veteran, husband and father, was also a great role model for a young boy. A doer, he was active in local veterans activities, his church and community functions. He worked for the Veteran's Administration rather than in private law practice because he had a passion for helping veterans struggling in civilian life.

I was in awe of him. He would come by our house with his own family yet always make time to focus individually on my sister and me. He'd ask what we were up to and his responses made us feel special. We loved him for caring. Years later we discovered we were not alone in our admiration of this man.

Complications from war injuries eventually mounted up

and he died too young. To the family's surprise, strangers arrived to attend his funeral service. Talking with them, we learned how really special my uncle was.

As far back as his family could remember he would go off Saturday mornings to, as he said, run errands. Back by mid afternoon, usually without packages, his family concluded this was his weekly "me" time. We discovered how wrong we were at his funeral.

In his VA work he'd hear of local veterans too injured, ill or aged to take care of routine home chores or even get groceries or medicines. Most didn't qualify for VA assistance and didn't have the resources to hire work done. When my uncle discovered their plight, he decided to personally help as many as he could. He spent every Saturday morning cutting grass, fixing things or running errands for people unable to do it themselves. Payment was refused but conversation was encouraged. He found many were alone with few people to talk to. As they relayed their stories each said my uncle had asked them not to tell anyone he was helping them saying, "I can't help everybody and I don't want others to feel sad if I don't reach them." My uncle lived the love principle. He cared about others and gave of himself with no thought of reward. In turn, those who knew him loved him.

My wife, like my uncle, is a follower of the love principle. When our daughters were teens, she took on leadership of a large regional church's teen group. Drawing from many communities, high schools and circumstances, the teens mixed successfully because of a basic membership requirement that insisted everyone be seen and treated as an equal. What a teen did in his or her community, at home or school had no bearing on who they were in this group. Teens considered nerds, popular, bullies or objects of bullies outside the group could be who they wanted to be in it. The operating principle was love in action. Activities were many and varied including social, sport, travel and musical events. Membership became so valued that, despite a strict behavior code, few teens challenged it except for an occasional innocent prank.

The church belonged to a national association that sponsored state, regional, and national teen conferences. Equality was stressed there as well. The success of this approach became obvious in an incident involving my youngest daughter.

A bright and capable child, she had a form of dyslexia that made traditional school programs painful. She was bright and learned easily but the restricting read-write-recite instructional approach of her school was nearly intolerable for her far more creative and expansive intellect. To compensate, she used free time to focus on her art skills. These were seldom appreciated or even acknowledged by the academically driven school staff. Things were different in the youth group.

The program at one multi-state regional conference included a talent show. When the list of participants was published, I noticed my daughter's name. It said she was going to perform a song from a new movie. I knew of her multiple talents but didn't know they included singing. I'd never heard her sing around the house. She later told me she wasn't confident of her singing ability so she only sang when no one else was around.

The night of the show she stepped on stage in front of several hundred teens and adults and began to sing. She was on pitch, phrased the music superbly, effectively captured the emotion of the lyrics and did it all in a strong melodic voice. The auditorium went silent as she began then erupted into thunderous applause as she finished. She was a sensation! Her self-image got a well-earned boost. I hugged and congratulated her after the performance asking where she found the courage to make her singing debut in front of such a large audience. Her answer was simple. "Dad, I knew I'd be safe here."

Those teens and adults shared a love that made it possible for any one of them to take a chance. It was the love that inspires someone to reach out and try something new.

Many religions and philosophies tell us there is a life principle that says we draw to us what we think about and give to others. If we feel a lack of love, it's time to ask, "Where is my thinking?" Am I timid and fearful around others? Am I critical of them? Do I feel superior or inferior to them? Do I see potential problems in relationships? A yes to any of these suggests we may be unconsciously driving away the love we seek. Fortunately we can change using a few basic techniques:

- **Being loved starts with being loving.** Train your mind to look at others as potential friends rather than problems. Avoid stereotypical thinking (people who are _____ are all _____). Stereotypes are at best exaggerations and at worst hurtful lies leading to rejection, bitterness and loss of opportunity. There's a reason for the Golden Rule "Do onto others as you would have others do unto you" mentioned in the Bible and other religions. It works!

- **Accept people as they are - warts and all.** This does not mean accepting inappropriate actions. If someone says or does something vulgar or dangerous, don't play Miss Manners and correct them. Simply remove yourself from the situation as tactfully as possible.

- **Care about others.** Offer help when it is clear help is needed. If they accept, you will have taken the first step toward developing a friendship.

- **Become aware of your body language.** Standing with arms crossed suggests a person who is closed to or intolerant of others. Frowning or looking away when someone looks at us says, "don't bother me." Tapping a foot, yawning or looking off into the distance when someone speaks to us says, "Your thoughts are not worth my time or attention."

- **Put shyness in its place.** Shyness is OK. Everyone is shy from time to time. Just don't let body language make things worse by communicating things you don't really feel. Appearing disinterested or aloof fairly screams, "Go away!"

- **When meeting people, show appreciation for them**. Smile and say hello first. A smile signals acceptance and hello is an overture to a brief conversation. If they ignore you, consider the possibility they may be shy or preoccupied and let them go. Chances are however, you'll receive a positive response.

The benefits of being loving often manifest in good and lasting friendships, the joy of being with family members, confidence working with other people and even finding a great life-long partner.

CHAPTER 11

You Can Age Gracefully

"I'm sorry," my grandfather would say, "You're five years old. The bottle clearly says 7Up. That means you have to be seven before you can drink this soda." He was teasing of course, but he stuck to his word. In retrospect, I realize he always had an ample supply of my favorite grape soda in the refrigerator. I recalled his little ritual while reviewing how my thoughts about aging have changed over the years.

As a child, I always wanted to be older. My first age target was five because at five I could go to this mysterious place called school just like my big sister. Seven was next. I would finally be able to drink the forbidden 7Up with grandpa. Then, I wanted to be eight so I could become a cub scout. Eleven meant I could be a boy scout. Fourteen meant high school and staying out with friends until nine or ten on non-school nights. At sixteen I could get a driver's license and have mobility. At twenty-one I would be an adult able to vote, drink alcohol and make my own decisions. When I was a youngster, age always meant ever increasing privileges.

I stopped thinking about age in my mid twenties. I was too busy with work and college. By thirty I was married and soon after a father. When I did think about growing older, it remained synonymous with things new. New experiences, new opportunities and new adventures came with every birthday.

At fifty, things started to change. Friends spoke negatively about age. Popular music, films, radio and television programs echoed this negative theme. TV commercials suggested growing older is synonymous with infirmity. According to them I would eventually need pharmaceutical help, life insurance, emergency monitoring products, walk-in baths and motorized wheel chairs to cope with incapacity. Some of my friends fought back by coloring their graying hair, plastering wrinkles with skin tightening creams, covering blemishes with cosmetics or going to the extreme of plastic surgery. I kept hearing I was getting old but darn, I didn't feel that way.

I finally decided to find out if there's an official time when a person is old. I read up on Social Security and found they and other retirement programs suggest people are old when they reach their mid sixties. That didn't seem right. I was still active in my sixties with older friends who were also active.

I asked my doctor. He said age is relative. He told me about a thirty-year-old whose body was suffering signs of old age due his lifestyle choices. He ate too much, refused to exercise, smoked a pack of cigarettes each day and consumed too much alcohol. Conversely, he said he had a patient in her eighties who acted and appeared to be twenty years younger. "There's no absolute measure as to when a person is old," he said. With this in mind, I decided to create my own idea of old age based on what I see around me. My measure suggests old age depends more on how a person lives rather than how many years.

As a hospital chaplain I'm privileged to talk to people of all ages. An eighty-one year-old man, who appeared no older than his mid fifties, told me he was president of a local hiking club. He even invited me to join one of his group's weekly walks. "We only go about ten miles," he reassured me. Suddenly, I felt old. He had no idea that in my present physical state, three miles would be more than I could comfortably handle. I was fifteen years his junior but at that moment I felt forty years older.

My many discussions with "young" old people confirm my view of aging. I really believe a person's age is related more to what's in their heads than the flipping of calendar pages. I now make it a point to ask particularly vital senior citizens what they think about aging.

One mid 80's woman said. "Aches and pains are on and off experiences throughout life and not just a sign of aging.

If an ache worries you see a doctor. If not, ignore it and move on. Don't dwell on what you don't want. Worrying makes you feel and act older than you are."

An elderly man told me the key to aging is simple. "Learn to live in harmony with your body. The notion you get what you give absolutely applies to aging," he added. "If you want to retain a measure of youthful vigor, eat wholesome foods in modest quantities, move your body regularly and care for your mind by including stimulating activities in your daily routine." He suggested taking regular walks around the neighborhood. "Talk with the people you meet," he said. "Go to community events, movies, parks, museums and other out of the home activities. Get into experiences that take you to an event at least once a week. Being active," he added, "helps get rid of boredom and makes you feel good."

One woman was adamant that people who complain about loneliness, isolation and depression simply haven't figured out people treat you the way you appear to them. "Shuffle along with your head down and you'll be treated like you're mentally or physically limited. Move briskly, greet people with a friendly smile and a hello and the chances are you'll at least get a smile and a quick return greeting back or even a conversation."

A number of elderly patients told me stressful thinking is a problem for many older folk. Having too much time on their hands, it seems causes many to take things like the daily news to heart. They worry about events and possibilities they would never have considered during their busy working and family raising years. They have a point. Physicians I talk to tell me needless worry shortens a person's life. Stress steals peace of mind and can causes our brain to call for the release of fight or flight chemicals in the body. When these chemicals are not immediately needed they can turn on and harm our bodies.

The best advice I got on peaceful living was to let things be as they are. Several people told me this is especially important when it comes to observing the misjudgments and mistakes of our adult children or friends. One woman said she learned the best thing she can do is to listen and make a comment only if she feels she must. "Mostly," she said, "let them learn from the consequences and challenges they create. It will mean more to them and you'll sleep better."

A 92 year-old woman told me, "Don't stew if your neighbor's noisy lawn mower or barking dog annoys you. Remember the noise is temporary. Put cotton in your ears or go somewhere else for a while. When we learn to ignore little annoyances, we live longer, healthier and are more fun to be around."

Several seniors mentioned cultivating talents. They observed everyone seems to be born with talents whether they know it or not. They suggested considering an urge to try something new such as singing, playing a musical instrument, woodworking, sewing or other interest a signal to do it.

One older artist told me he didn't get into art until his seventies. On a whim, he took a stained glass course at a local high school's adult education program. He loved working with glass and found out he was good at it. He took his new skills and began creating quirky humorous pieces that sold well at art and craft shows. Before long he had achieved local notoriety. He said he eventually joined the local glass art guild where he was welcomed.

A lifelong bachelor, he said he'd spent fifty years as a movie theater projectionist. Isolated by the solitary nature of his work. He never married and had few friends. Then came retirement. He suddenly had time to discover things he'd been missing. When he found his talent for making glass objects, he also discovered the joy of having people in his life. Eyes watering, he said he considered the guild's older members the siblings he never had and the younger ones his adopted children. "My senior years." he said, "are the happiest of my life."

Aging gracefully it appears, only requires a willingness to get out of the easy chair and join others in the world. It is doing not withering away in solitude. It is cherishing friends and loved ones, finding joy in daily activities, limiting unnecessary worry, being grateful for what we have and looking forward to tomorrow's surprises.

CHAPTER 12

Send Your Inner Critic Packing

I'd be willing to bet everyone at one time or another has had the thought "I'm not good enough." It's the work of an inner critic each of us carries inside us. It is especially active at times when we feel insecure. All inner critics have one thing in common. Their words are almost always untrue.

Born in childhood, an inner critic survives by feeding on misunderstanding, mistakes, and the unkind comments of others. Allowed to run free in the subconscious, it erodes self-confidence and limits opportunities for success.

My oldest daughter ran headlong into this monster in middle school. An excellent student, she found herself struggling to grasp the algebra principles presented in her eighth grade math class. Her inner critic told her she was just not good at math and she believed it. Fortunately her teacher didn't. When she told him she couldn't do Algebra he told her she was wrong and he could prove it. "Your belief is due to a misunderstanding not a lack of ability," he told her. "You believe math gets harder as you go along. It doesn't. Problems just get longer." He showed her how algebra combines multiple math operations into single problems. "Solving them," he added, "merely requires dividing problems into units and working on them one unit at a time." He did several with her then had her work through others. Before long she was handling Algebra with ease. Confidence in her math skills was restored and her critic spewing a false belief, was put into her mental trash bin.

Correcting a child's math misunderstanding is easy compared to discarding an inner critic's favorite source of anxiety and misery, the notion we are what we do. How this thinking comes about can be traced back to childhood.

When we are children, parents, relatives, friends, acquaintances and even teachers often innocently refer to us as good or bad girls and boys equating behavior with value. Unfortunately, these kinds of comments give children the impression they are what they do. The truth is, humans are far more complex and interesting than a simple statement like that implies. But, children, don't know this. They accept at face value false good/bad notions thus birthing an inner critic ready to control their thinking. Over time, this false good/bad notion can make us fearful of making mistakes. This is sad. It over looks the fact mistakes can be incredibly helpful. Mistakes inspire people to search for workable alternatives.

The late Boston Red Sox baseball slugger Ted Williams was not always the award winning hitter he came to be. He once told a reporter he developed his remarkable hitting ability only after he realized fear of striking out was holding him back. He said when he decided to tune out the fear of missing the ball and concentrate instead on what the ball was doing as it approached home plate something amazing happened. The ball seemed to slow down as it came toward him. He could actually see how the seams were rotating and thus have an idea as to whether it was a fastball, curveball, slider etc. Many hitting titles and accolades resulted from ignoring his inner critic long enough to know where and when to swing the bat.

Mistakes are not the problem. Criticism outside and inside us is. I was fortunate to have a wonderful boss who hated criticism. He made it clear he didn't mind honest mistakes. All he asked was that he be among the first to hear about them along with our understanding as to why it happened and what we planned to do about it. He was adamant no blame was to be assigned. He just expected us to do what was needed and ask for help if we wanted it.

Criticism is a stressor. It brings on fatigue and lessens our ability to perform in the future. Fortunately, it can be managed with a few simple acts that essentially kick out or control our inner critic.

If an inner critic is causing stress in you, try taking a me break. A 'me' break can be a minute, an hour, a day or a vacation. It is a time to recall accomplishments, activities, people, places and things that make you feel good about yourself. It's time to recognize you are a valuable human being. Sure, you make mistakes but you're also creative and capable of great accomplishments.

Coffee used to be my excuse for a 'me' break. I stopped getting it from a coffee pot near my office so I could take a few minutes to walk down to the coffee service in the building lobby. The five-minute round trip gave me just enough time to take stock of problems, accomplishments, objectives and to say hello to a colleague or two in another department. I returned to my office refreshed. This simple routine left my inner critic looking for me in the lobby and out of my hair.

Periodically take a few minutes to remind yourself you are a valuable, talented individual. You have skills and talents that are different and often better than others. If you feel you haven't found them yet, no problem. Do some exploring based on what you enjoy in addition to what you feel you must do. Most of all ignore your inner critic or better still, send him or her packing. You need motivation not criticism.

CHAPTER 13

Watch What You Say, It Matters

"I'm sick and tired of your bickering!" the exasperated mother said to her children. Sure enough, within minutes she was sick and tired with a miserable headache. Without knowing it, she had activated a creative power she wasn't aware she possessed. She didn't know we each have the power to make real what we declare with intensity and it doesn't matter whether the declaration is positive or negative. The trigger words are I am. Upon hearing them, our mind accepts they represent something we want in our life. Notice I said "in our life." What we create may impact the world but its greatest impact will always be on us.

Successful artists, writers, actors, musicians and athletes are adept at using this power. They visualize an objective, get to work and before long it becomes at least a temporary reality.

Method actors make their characters come alive on stage by temporarily stepping into the persona of the individual they are playing. They declare they are their character so they can experience appropriate feelings and reactions. Show business stories abound about actors so into this technique they have difficulty dropping their character when stepping off stage.

When you think about it, aren't we all method actors to some extent? When we wake each morning we're probably as true to the person we really are as we will be all day. Once out of bed we assume roles like mother, father, son, daughter, brother, sister, employee, boss etc. We leave the house and step into still other roles like driver, rider, pedestrian, student, lawyer, worker, plumber, clerk or teacher. Each time we take on a new role, and we often do this several times a day, we temporarily set aside the others. This is our mind's creativity in action.

I began today as a husband. Now I'm a writer. By afternoon I'll be a grandfather, friend or whatever else I choose or need to be. I slip seamlessly between roles whenever I think, "I am _____." This remarkable power is intriguing, even fun, but it must be used carefully. Saying it unwisely can lead to an unpleasant result. Saying, "I am tired," can make us weary. Saying. "I am dumb," can dull our mental faculties. Saying, "I am clumsy," can cause us to stumble into an accident. The potential for unpleasant consequences from negative thought is reason enough to strive to be as positive as we can.

My wife is an artist. She creates astonishingly beautiful

works in glass and with textiles. But it wasn't until she declared herself to be an artist that her work began to take off. She started in art thinking "I want to be an artist." With experience she declared herself an artisan (a skilled art worker but not yet a creator). When her work began to win awards and sell, she felt comfortable declaring herself to be an artist! Interest in her work soared.

Saying "I may be" or "I want to be," communicates uncertainty about a desire. It leaves our creative powers unclear about what to do. Committing to a thought and taking appropriate action is what makes things happen. Fortunately, our actions are alterable. When the young mother's headache appeared, she could have declared, "I feel better" and reinforced her intention by taking an aspirin.

As children we are not usually experienced or mature enough to function effectively on our own. Feeling a need for protection and guidance, we unconsciously surrender much life control to parents, teachers, family and other authority figures. Our creative power is always present however.

As we develop experience-based judgment, we depend less on others and more on our own thinking. This is the life period when we also learn choices have consequences.

Thoughtful adults intuitively recognize there is power in their words and thoughts. Through them they direct the events that rule their lives. This is not to say the unexpected can be avoided. Surprises are also a part of living. The unexpected does not have to rule however.

We can use our creative powers to take control and direct our responses appropriately. We can choose the reaction we prefer: "I am able to handle this." "I am not going to be a victim." "I will succeed."

Keep in mind what we declare can also make a situation worse; "I am afraid," "I can't handle this." "It's unfair." These thoughts tell our creative powers what to produce. It takes positive thoughts to bring positive results.

Watching what we say is wisdom in action. Think before making a declaration. Avoid hasty decisions where possible. Stay positive. Always remember, when we declare something using words like "I am..." we are creating elements of our future like them or not. If your desire is for good, make "I will watch what I say" a guiding phrase in you life.

CHAPTER 14

Does Prayer Really Work?

The pain in my side was sharp and constant. Thinking it was the flu, I suffered two days before seeing a doctor. When I finally went to her office, the diagnosis was immediate - appendicitis. Appendicitis! I couldn't believe it. I was 49 years old. "Isn't appendicitis a childhood illness?" I asked. The doctor shook her head no as she instructed an assistant to rush me by wheel chair from her office in the hospital's professional building to the emergency center next door. A surgeon was called; I was prepped, placed on a gurney and moving toward the operating room when I became violently ill. I later learned that was likely the point at which my appendix ruptured. Surgery was performed and procedures started to contain the toxins released by the rupture. I awoke in a recovery area to find large tubes attached to gurgling machines sticking out of my abdomen and multiple packs of intravenous fluids running through a smaller tube in my arm.

The surgeon told me the operation was successful but toxins released by the rupture were now swirling around my internal organs. High-powered antibiotics were being administered to control infection and a flushing procedure was in place to force the toxins out of my body. He said my task was to rest and permit the procedures to work. All went well until the third day following surgery.

I became exhausted, clammy, sweaty and cold. My temperature soared. I then realized I could die from this experience. Hospital staff were doing what they could but my condition continued to worsen. I instinctively knew survival demanded I do something. Prayer seemed my best alternative.

Seeking privacy and quiet, I asked my wife to help me into the lavatory. With her help, I eased off the bed and into the room with my IV pole and hardware in tow. I shut the door, sat on the closed commode, became quiet and silently shouted, "I will not die! I will be with my children as they grow up!" I repeated these thoughts over and over with increasing intensity. Exhausted, I finally fell silent while leaning against the cold tiled wall. Almost immediately I sensed the words, go walk! They were stated gently and repeated several times before I grasped I was hearing them. I knew what to do. I flung open the door and announced, "I'm going for a walk."

My wife's expression told me she thought I was delirious. It didn't matter. I was going for a walk! Seeing my determination, she took one arm as I hung onto the intravenous drip pole with the other and we slowly moved out into the hallway. It didn't take many steps for exhaustion to send me back to bed. I lay there for a while then announced, "I'm going to walk again." This time my walk lasted a little longer before exhaustion again forced a stop. I repeated this trek and rest routine several times eventually making it most of the way down the hall and back.

I felt better after my last walk. A nurse arrived to check my vital signs. Finishing, she looked at me in amazement. "Everything's normal," she stammered. My fever had broken. The infection was apparently under control. I grew stronger each of the next five days and was then released.

A check-up at the surgeon's office a week following my hospital release revealed everything was healing well and my vitals remained normal. Finishing his examination, he looked at me for a moment then said, "I have to ask. Why did you start walking at the hospital?" I said simply, it seemed like a good idea at the time. He looked at me questioningly then said, "You should know your walks likely saved your life. You were receiving the most powerful antibiotic available yet the toxins kept gaining ground. You were dying and there seemed nothing we could do. Nurses were praying for you. Then you started walking. As best we can determine, your walks kicked your body's immune system into high gear and it, in combination with the antibiotics, knocked out the infection. Your experience is as close to a miracle as I've ever seen."

In retrospect, I'm convinced my survival was the result of prayer in action – others and mine. I was in crisis and needed more than medicine could provide. I became quiet and forcefully made known my desire believing I was connecting to a power greater than myself. In moments I received the direction, go walk! I understood and got into action.

We hear about prayer from an early age but few of us seem to understand its function and power. I choose to see it as a vehicle through which we consciously connect to the intelligence that is the source of existence. Some call it God. Others refer to it as Allah, Yahweh, Elohim, Bhagavan and so on. Whatever the name, I'm convinced prayer is a way to connect to it and through this connection change lives.

Weeks later, mulling over my experience, I remembered I'd seen this phenomenon before. My mother, long steeped in spirituality, used the same connection to achieve a similar result.

Diagnosed with an aggressive form of breast cancer at age sixty-four, she took charge of her situation. Following a double mastectomy, she was told the cancer in her body had spread to her lymph nodes and was no longer controllable. The doctor said the life expectancy of patients in her condition was often between three and six months. Momentarily devastated, she took a deep breath looked the doctor in the eye and said, "Not in my case!" My wife was pregnant with our first child. My sister had two children born a few years earlier. My wife and I planned to eventually have a second child. With these children in mind, my mother told the doctor she was not about to die until she had gotten to know all of her grandchildren including my two yet to be born. She was adamant. She asked him to do the best he could with chemotherapy and radiation then added, "I will also request help from a higher source."

My mother lived seven years beyond the dreaded diagnosis before succumbing to the disease. She believed prayer and her will to live supported by science would take care of her. She succeeded. She knew all four or her grandchildren before she moved on.

Does prayer work? I believe it does especially when combined with powerful intention, action and support from others. Prayer helps us focus life energy in ways that support our intentions and desires. Whether ill or not, I urge you to get into a prayer routine.

Start sessions by becoming conscious of the presence of a profound intelligence (God). Don't try to form a picture. Focus instead on an all loving, all powerful, all knowing and ever present source of positive energy and enlightenment.

Request help with any problem or concern troubling you. State your intention. Ask for the help then stop! You don't have to repeat a prayer request over and over. Just believe you've been heard and are being supported.

Prayer awakens creative powers already in us. Add physical actions such as visiting a doctor or others whose skills can be helpful and we put into motion elements and powers we cannot begin to imagine. We may be spiritual beings but here, we are having a human experience in a physical world. A doctor and medicine, can play a vital role in answering a healing prayer. Bankers, tradespersons and others can do the same in their skill areas.

Give thanks AND get into action. When you make a prayer request, picture yourself as you wish to be. Release fear, doubt and concern. If you find this difficult, ask for additional help by praying, "I believe! Now please, help me with my disbelief."

CHAPTER 15

I Can't Do It

The thought of doing something and possibly looking foolish or failing can so frighten us we become convinced we can't do it.

Our youngest daughter was an example of this thinking while still a toddler. She became so comfortable as a three year old she grew concerned about growing older. On the eve of her fourth birthday she announced she did not want and would not accept turning four. She was satisfied where she was, thank you very much. Her birthday arrived despite protests and she soon found herself surrounded by family, friends, fun, gifts and yummy treats. She reconsidered. The next day she proclaimed growing older is OK! Her three-year-old viewpoint blocked her ability to grasp the good that lay ahead. Fortunately a dose of birthday fun was all she needed to change her mind. It's not usually that easy for most of us.

As a teacher I ran into this problem several times a year. A student would do poorly on a test. Frustrated and embarrassed, they'd decide they just didn't have the ability to learn the subject matter and stop working. They were wrong of course, and a little coaching from teachers and friends soon got them to realize it.

Our mind accepts what we believe and directs our creative nature to make it real. A planned outdoor activity cancelled due to rain can be viewed two ways. Viewed negatively, it can lead to a day of moping around over a lost opportunity. Viewed positively, it can be seen as a freedom from responsibilities day and lead to unplanned fun.

Saying or thinking "I can't," is a great way to self-sabotage. Fortunately we can change the scenario by thinking, "I am bright and capable of doing whatever I declare." Our mind moves us to make beliefs true. As individuals the way we achieve that good depends on our mental and physical capabilities. This means we may not all do things the same way.

I experienced a wonderful example of this first hand when visiting a school program for physically impaired youngsters. A blind from birth elementary school student challenged me to a basketball shoot out in the gym. "The one who sinks the most baskets in three minutes," he declared, "will be the winner." I couldn't imagine how he could win but I didn't want to discourage him. I went first and missed more than I sank. When he stepped up to shoot he put ball after ball through the hoop. Stunned, I asked how he did it. His and answer was simple and direct. "I may not be able to see," he explained, "but I have good ears. I use them instead." He said he learned to tell where the ball was on the court by listening for its bouncing echo off the walls of the gym. Since he knew where the basket is from past experience, he then knew when and where to place his shot. Admittedly I'm not very good at basketball but this youngster was amazing. Faced with a problem and belief in his ability to solve it, his mind translated his working sensory input into appropriate body actions.

Many so-called disabled people use the power of belief to achieve fame and fortune. I was captivated watching deaf musician Evelyn Glennie conduct a world-class symphony orchestra playing a complicated selection. She said she could feel the instrument vibrations and use them to guide her. Entertainers Whoopi Goldberg and Jay Leno both overcame dyslexia, a malady that causes the mind to jumble letters in words. Actor James Earl Jones (the voice of Darth Vader in the Star Wars movies and a performer in numerous films, plays and TV commercials) was a serious stutterer until he decided to overcome it and did. Over and over successful people tell of deciding they can do something then going out and doing it. Using a combination of belief, grit and determination, they achieve what at first seemed impossible.

We all can use our minds to achieve things when we

believe we can. What about desiring to do something physically impossible? Can we really believe ourselves into doing it?

Well, unless you're Superman, leaping a tall building at a single bound, racing a locomotive or being immune to a speeding bullet may seem impossible for a human. But are these things really impossible?

Engineers at Alternative Technologies, Inc. created a small inexpensive strap-on one-man helicopter that can take off from and return to a tight space. It can lift an individual over very tall objects and return them safely to ground. So much for a man or woman not being able to leap tall buildings at a single bound.

Racing a locomotive is a snap for someone in one of today's speedy single person transportation devices that operate on land, in the air and on water.

Du Pont chemist Stephanie Kwolek wanted to protect soldiers, police officers and others from being harmed by bullets. Believing she could find a way, she experimented with chemicals and materials until she created Kevlar. It stops bullets and other life threatening objects such as knives. Since it's creation, Kevlar has been used to save the lives of thousands of soldiers and police officers worldwide. Stop a speeding bullet? Done!

Admittedly, these feats were not accomplished the way Superman did them in comic books, but the results were the same. All it took was belief and dedication by their creators.

What's next? Dick Tracy's wrist radio? Well... if you think about it... the Apple iWatch is doing that and more.

We make dreams real when we turn a desire into a belief and follow up with physical effort. Will we be or create the best something in the world? Perhaps yes, perhaps no. But one thing is sure. We'll never achieve much of anything until we believe we can.

I would be remiss if I didn't point out the opposite of belief based creativity is also true. Believing we can't do something tells our mind and body to make that belief true. What we belief affects our confidence and creativity. Say it enough and we permit fear, regret, illness and misery to take control of us. A belief is a self-fulfilling prophecy. Make it negative and you lose.

Correcting an I can't belief requires opening our minds to at least the possibility we might, with time and effort, be able to achieve something we desire. We deal with doubt by appreciating what we have done and can do. Making a list of our accomplishments small and large and reading it when an "I can't" thought shows up may help.

Success comes to those who know what they want, believe they can have it and get to work. Bill Gates (Microsoft) failed in his first computer effort. Harlan Sanders, founder of Kentucky Fried Chicken, was rejected 1,009 times before becoming successful. Both of these individuals believed in what they were doing, kept making adjustments and ultimately achieved their desires. You can too!

CHAPTER 16

Be Afraid?

Cancer! Me? My mind was focused on this question as my wife and I entered the doctor's office to hear lab results. His demeanor provided the answer before a word was spoken. I had cancer. He reassured us it was treatable and could likely be eliminated through one of several options. He gave us literature, answered questions then sent us home to decide what to do. Days of indecision and fear passed before we chose the surgical option. The procedure was done in 2001 without complications. I have now been cancer free for over sixteen years.

I think about this experience whenever I hear someone speak about fear. Fear is a natural feeling. It 's useful in motivating us to action when serious illness, crime, weather or natural disasters strike. Unfortunately, fear can also be used to manipulate us to buy goods, services or ideas. Newscasters, talk show hosts, politicians, interest groups, businesses and even some religious leaders use fear in this way.

Fear as motivator is not new. Ancient texts acknowledge and denounce it. The Bible, for example, urges people to resist fear-filled thoughts more than 300 times. It asks people to replace fear with righteous thoughts and actions.

In his book, "Conversations with God," author Neale Donald Walsch, uses an acronym to describe fear. He suggests more often than not fear is merely false evidence appearing real (F.E.A.R). He suggests we internalize this definition and apply it to circumstances that make us fearful. A good way to lesson fear's power is to become aware of the techniques used by truth manipulators.

If you hear someone encouraging us versus them thinking, be wary. This is an ages old fear generating technique intended to place a mental barrier between people. Nationality, race, color, financial status, type of work, education, political orientation, religion and gender are the most used and abused characteristics. If a fear builder can get us to hunker down behind one or more of these barriers he or she can limit our thinking and direct our actions toward his or her specific goals. A typical example is to make an outrageous statement sound reasonable. All people who: (you pick the verb - are, do, think, act. look like, etc. - are _____ you pick the claim) is a typical example. The truth is all people are never the same no matter what some may like to think.

Another technique is to anticipate terrible things that could result from a situation, event or action even though such result is unlikely or even impossible. Had I spent time between my cancer diagnosis and treatment focused on negative possibilities, I might have succumbed to indecision and delayed treatment until cure was not possible. Fear held in thought has a way of producing fearful results often unrelated to the projected cause.

Advertising has mastered the art of fear-based motivation. Under the cloak of being helpful, cosmetic firms play on our fear of rejection by others (body odor, blemishes, hair color, etc.) to sell soaps, deodorants, creams and more. Clothing, automobiles, appliances, homes and other products are promoted on the promise they will positively impress others making us appear important. Newspapers, radio, TV and Internet forums are filled with fear notions to garner attention, motivate us to stay tuned, take specific actions or contribute to a cause.

Be afraid? Maybe. But understand fear is a product of anticipation and imagination. Fear may be good when we're faced with an immediate physical danger such as a lion in the wild looking for dinner, but it's not so good when we permit others to use it control us.

A better response to fear is to pause before acting. Pausing gives our thinking/reasoning abilities time to determine if what we are hearing, reading or seeing might really be false information appearing real.

Accepting other's ideas, suggestions or actions without first determining their truth, surrenders control of our lives to them. They may sound good at the moment but with reflection we may discover they limit desirable experiences and opportunities and put us into risk rather than protect us from harm. This is why many voters suffer from post election remorse.

Be afraid when there is verifiable evidence of a need (e.g. weather alerts) and take appropriate action. But never blindly give your life and safety over to the control of others because of what they say or do. New technology makes it possible for unscrupulous individuals to manipulate photos, videos, film and audio recordings in ways that make the unreal look real. Charismatic speakers can make convincing arguments until their facts are carefully checked. History tells us the consequences of acting on emotion rather than thought. Many an oppressive dictator took power by making people feel he was benevolent. Unnecessary wars have been fought based on hearsay. In the words of the late historian and moralist John Acton, "Power tends to corrupt, and absolute power corrupts absolutely."

Feelings of fear unaccompanied by an immediate physical cause fairly scream it is time for thought. Consider checking unfamiliar truth claims using reliable sources such as Fact Checker and Snopes on the Internet, reading newspapers and magazines that base their stories on reporters in the field following the action.

We control fear by taking personal responsibility for our thoughts. Listen to others but make decisions based on personal thoughts and/or the thoughts of others with a track record of accuracy.

CHAPTER 17

Are You Nervous Around Others?

Elementary school was a mix of fun, boredom and harassment by other kids. I held my own until junior high when I discovered girls were more than pests. I wanted to impress them but didn't know how. Afraid of appearing foolish and clumsy, I held back. This of course made me appear foolish and clumsy.

Things improved a bit in high school. I got an after school job at the local radio station where I became an early evening top 40 disc jockey. Coaching from veteran broadcasters helped me develop an effective on-air personality. Being outgoing on the radio was easy. I had a microphone and a whole radio station between the listeners and me. Radio notoriety did make me a little more outgoing at school but inside I remained insecure in relating to people on a one to one basis.

I covered my social insecurity in college by acting like the person I wanted to be. Out of college I met the wonderful girl who became my wife. I had a good job and, I thought, a fairly positive self-image. Unfortunately my insecurity returned at important moments. My wife still teases me over the fact I asked her to marry me three different times just to be sure she really meant yes.

I eventually got insecurity under control. I held good jobs, raised a family, and appeared comfortable with others. Still, I was never totally at ease until I discovered the secret to relaxing around others.

When I retired from education following a thirty-four year career, I pursued my lifelong interest in spirituality by training as a minister then hospital chaplain. Through these people to people roles I learned the magic path to comfort and security with other people.

Ministers and chaplains are often called upon to deal with people in crisis. Effectiveness requires compassion, caring, empathy and the ability to comfortably relate to others. I was responsible for initiating conversations and following up with give and take discussions.

It didn't take long to discover the secret to being comfortable with other people is to focus on them not you. When I concentrated on others, conversation became easy. It was no longer important what someone might think of me.

I focused on them and their needs. Making this adjustment did two things. I stopped thinking about my feelings and they responded positively to me. After all, who doesn't like someone who cares about them?

Today, I'm seldom self-conscious with others. I initiate conversations freely and am often rewarded with enjoyable chats. One of my adult daughters brought this to my attention on a recent shopping trip. "I can't believe the number of people who talk to you," she said. "I bet most of them would tell you their entire life story if you gave them the time." For a guy who wasted so much of his life being timid around others, her observation was gratifying.

Mulling over my daughter's comment, I realized everyone can do what I do. It becomes automatic with practice. Feeling nervous and insecure around other people is simply the result of not understanding how to relate. Putting the focus on them is key but there are things you can do to make that process easier. Here is what I do. I won't guarantee you'll be the life of the party but I am sure you'll enjoy the party more than ever before:

- **Suggestion one** - Smile... a lot. When you smile at others, you visually tell them you like and accept them as they are. With so much criticism and so little appreciation prevalent in today's world, a smile is a most welcome gesture.

- **Suggestion two** - Speak first. You don't have to make a speech. Simply say hello or ask someone what he or she thinks of the weather. Their reaction will likely earn you a return comment with a nod and a word or two. I find most people want to be friendly. They may not want a lengthy conversation but they will respond when they feel their response will be welcomed. If they ignore you, oh well - nothing ventured nothing gained. Don't take it personally. They may be having a difficult time or just a busy day.

- **Suggestion three** - Maintain boundaries. Being friendly does not license you to intrude on someone's privacy. Neither does it mean taking on their burdens or permitting them into your personal life. Take your clue from their responses. They may not be in the mood for chitchat or they may become too chatty. Don't allow them take advantage of your friendliness. You are your own person with your own challenges. If someone seems to be misinterpreting your overture, politely and immediately set things straight by suggesting they look into other resources that can help them.

- **Suggestion four** - Find the joy others have for you. Everyone has a story. If it seems appropriate and you have the time, ask people about their interests and lives. Let them share experiences with you. Follow their comments with a question or some interesting or amusing tidbit about you that relates to what they've said. Be careful not to brag and bore them. Great conversations start with curiosity and end with a mutually enjoyable experience.

- **My last suggestion** - Relax and be you. You are a wonderful human being with ideas and experiences that will likely fascinate others. Let go of concern about what they think of you. Just don't haul out a slew of travel or family photos. Simply picture yourself talking to an old friend with whom you're comfortable and don't need to impress. Who knows, you may be talking to your next good friend.

CHAPTER 18

Create the Life You Want

Are you living the life you want? If so, congratulations. If not, it's time to do something about it. Dreams stay dreams until they're translated into action. We do this with goals and an action plan. The process sounds simple but as you get into it you'll find it more interesting and intriguing than you can imagine. Creating the life you want begins with a commitment. If you're ready to change your life, grab a few sheets of paper, a pen or pencil and let's get to work.

Begin by writing a short paragraph that sums up what you want. Include examples of things, experiences, people and events you desire.

Now write a brief list of jobs, family situations, type of home, travel experiences, financial state, friends, possessions and so on you feel will give you what you want. When this is done, it's time to consider what you must do to get them.

On another sheet of paper write what you think it will take to achieve them. What training or education, experiences, finances, health, relocations or other requirements will be needed. If you want to be an electrician, lawyer, teacher or business tycoon for example, what will it take to do these things? You can get most of this information through Internet searches and some soul searching.

Review what you've written then ask yourself, "Am I willing to do what it takes to do this?" Cross out any that no longer interest you.

Next, prioritize the items on the list. Place your most desired item at the top and add others in order of most to least desired. Spend time on this. Think through the effect each item will have on your life. Be certain you understand what impact it may have on your relationships, energy, location, time and money.

Now ask yourself, "Do I really believe I can do and have the things I've listed?" Putting items on a list does not make them happen. It takes work, time and belief that you can do it. Keep in mind, the single most important factor keeping people from the life they want is failure to believe they can have it.

A high school football player wanted to be the team kicker. He read up on placekicking. He knew exactly what to do but when he actually tried kicking, the result was the ball going short or wide of the goal post. His coach took him aside and told him he believed he had the skill to be a kicker but he was trying too hard to do too much. He asked him to quit trying to kick 40-yard field goals and instead kick them from the 10-yard line. Before long the young man was consistently making 10-yard kicks. The coach then moved him back to the 15-yard line then the 20 and so on. He eventually was kicking 45-yard field goals consistently. The young man didn't change his kicking technique but he did change his belief. He was able to kick long goals because, through experience, he honed his skills and adopted the belief he could do it.

If a major goal seems too difficult, do what the footballer did. Make a series of progressive goals you can believe in and move one goal at a time to where you want to be. It will take work and time but you'll eventually realize how easy it is to be successful when you "know" you can be.

As you work toward something, remind yourself why you included the goal on your list. You believed then you could accomplish it. You may have had unexpected bumps, surprises and challenges. But are they reason enough to change your opinion? If so, change your goal. If not set fear aside and remember past accomplishments. Remind yourself how good each accomplishment felt. You have met challenges before and won. If you really want something dismiss doubt. Feel the fear then go ahead and create the life you want even if it takes longer than expected. Millions of people accomplish things that seemed impossible to them daily. Be the millions plus one and enjoy your victory.

CHAPTER 19

Dealing with A Loss

He had a long loving marriage; a caring family and so many friends attending his funeral they over-filled the room. His wife maintained composure throughout the service. She chatted with people and graciously accepted condolences. I watched and noticed something behind her demeanor. As the minister selected to conduct the service, I suggested we chat later in the week. She agreed but didn't respond to my follow-up call. A few weeks later I ran into her at a local grocery store. She looked terrible. Again I suggested a chat. This time, we met.

She told me her life had been a whirl of activity since the funeral. She then burst into tears and stammered, "I'm furious with him. I don't want to be angry, but I am. My husband always handled our finances, house and car maintenance.

Now I have to do these things and I don't know what I'm doing. I'm scared and mad and it makes me feel guilty. I know he didn't leave me by choice. I know he wouldn't want me to be overburdened, but I am and I just can't help being furious with him for putting me in this position."

I assured her anger and guilt are standard parts of the grieving process. The fact they'd been married 60 years added intensity. I suggested lessening or eliminating these feelings is a challenge for most people following the death of a spouse. It's not an overnight task but in most cases, anger lessens with time. The healing process begins by recognizing these feelings are normal.

Her husband left her financially secure so I suggested she consider turning overwhelming tasks, at least initially, over to professionals such as accountants, lawyers and handymen. I also advised reaching out to close friends and family with whom she feels comfortable talking about her feelings.

Almost everyone recognizes feelings of loss by survivors following the death of a loved one are normal. But few realize these feelings are not limited to deaths. Life-altering events of any kind can bring on similar grief. The loss of a job, a financial reversal, a forced relocation, a divorce, victim of a crime, an unexpected illness or a serious injury are other grief prompting examples.

Reactions to grief vary on an individual basis. Lists of them are available through many psychology groups. Few people experience all of them but knowing they exist can soften their impact when they do strike. Here are a few typical loss reactions:

- **Denial** is a common feeling. Many people are not ready to accept the reality of a death or change in circumstances. They feel what happened cannot be real or they may try to avoid thinking about it at all.

- **Guilt** frequently accompanies feelings of anger. This happens when we feel we shouldn't be angry as in the case of the death of a loved one. .

- **Resentment** may form if we feel we don't deserve what's happening to us. It often accompanies anger and guilt.

- **Despair** may come as we face a life significantly different from our past. It is easy to feel everything we hoped for is ruined.

- **Anxiety** is tied to fear. It occurs when we know we cannot keep doing what we've done yet we don't know what to do.

- **Emptiness and isolation** comes with a feeling of being alone with a crisis. It's easy to think we may never love, work or enjoy life again.

- **Depression** frequently inspires the feeling nothing matters anymore.

- **Loss of Identity** is also a common reaction. It occurs not just with a death but also in people who have lost or retired from a job. We used to be a husband, wife, boss, leader, famous, etc. but now we don't know who we are.

- **Illness** is a form of withdrawal from life. Psychosomatic and/or physical symptoms and ailments appear.

- **Anger and blaming** is not unusual. Emotions flare when we feel we've been put into circumstances we don't deserve. We want to blame someone or something. This is particularly common where death, divorce or loss of a job is involved.

It is human nature to blame when we experience loss. It makes us feel better, at first. Over time however it almost always proves to be counterproductive. Blaming holds on to negativity that can blind us to future possibilities. Forgiveness has proven to be a better approach. Forgiveness releases responsibility for the past enabling us to move beyond a problem.

If blaming is a problem, foster forgiving by finding a quiet place with a comfortable chair. Once settled, think about whoever or whatever needs forgiving, including yourself.

Hold them in mind and say in thought or out loud, (name of individual) is released from responsibility for (reason). This activity may seem like it's for others but it's actually just for us. Forgiveness helps us release anger, frustration and anxiety. It opens our mind and heart for new acquaintances, friends, colleagues, activities and joys. Spiritually inclined individuals often find comfort, support and guidance through meditation and prayer.

Sharing feelings with others can help when we've experienced a loss. Find a friend, support group, counselor or clergyperson who will listen and only occasionally provide a suggestion or support. Many hospitals and churches have such groups. Whomever we chose as a confidant, it must be someone who makes us feel safe and comfortable expressing thoughts and feelings. Putting our thoughts "out there" helps us see, recognize and deal with the emotions we are experiencing.

Getting past a loss requires accepting the fact circumstances have changed. We can't safely drive a car forward looking primarily in the rearview mirror. Similarly, we can't move forward in life constantly looking to the past. Old feelings and thoughts don't have to be forgotten just stored in memory to be brought out occasionally. We must make room for new thoughts.

A loss may force us to take on new responsibilities, develop new skills or even relocate leaving behind people and surroundings that made us comfortable. Realizing our life will never be the same is unnerving. Fortunately human beings have the ability to adapt, change, and again find joy. The requirement is that we take control of what is happening to us.

CHAPTER 20

Look for the Joy

Life lessons often come to us in ways we could never predict. I received one through an 85-year-old roommate when I was hospitalized recovering from appendix surgery.

A long time cardiac patient, his latest problem was restricted blood flow in his legs due to collapsing arteries. The situation was so severe gangrene had begun to occur. I overheard his doctor tell him and family members, "Your age and physical condition is such we can't use surgery to correct the problem and medicines are not proving effective. All we can do is make you comfortable and let nature take its course." My roommate turned to his family and said, "Darlings I've been blessed with a great wife, a great family and life. Whatever lies ahead is in God's hands. I know I'll be OK."

I had been feeling sorry for myself due to hospital confinement. Hearing his words however, I realized my attitude was selfish and unreasonable. Here was my less healthy roommate taking bad news in stride and encouraging those around him to do the same.

I then noticed he was always cheerful and positive. He was thankful for hospital staff efforts on his behalf. I finally asked how he managed to stay so up. He looked at me with a smile and said, "Years ago I discovered life is a series of downs and ups. If you take downs too seriously you become so miserable you miss the ups and that just makes you more miserable. I didn't want to be miserable so I began to look for the ups."

"It took me a while," he went on, "but I finally figured out life is a lot more fun when I quit fussing about things beyond my control." He told me this attitude started years ago when he was working on an assembly line at one of Detroit's auto plants. His job was installing tires on the left side of new cars. It was hot heavy work. "I got through each day," he said, "by thinking about the people who would buy each car. If I was working on a sedan, I pictured a family. If it was a two-door model, I pictured a salesman. If it was a convertible, I saw a young person. I decided then and there each buyer was going to receive the best-installed left side tires I could give them. Thinking like this made me feel good and the job didn't seem so tough anymore. I found joy in my job and that made all the difference in how I felt."

MANAGE YOUR LIFE

I asked if he really believed there is joy in all situations. He said yes. "OK," I responded, "where's the joy in being hospitalized?" He paused, gave me a long look then said, "Have you really looked around my friend. We have nurses, doctors, aides, technicians, dietitians, cleaners and others tending to our every need day and night. Doesn't being surrounded by people who care about you bring at least a little smile to your heart?"

True to his word, he spent his days appreciating the attention he received. He shared stories and jokes. He didn't complain even when tests and treatments were painful. He refused to dwell on his illness lest he miss some of the good things around him. I asked if his behavior was religiously inspired. He laughed and said, "I've never been religious other than to go to church at Christmas and Easter when my wife made me do it. I don't dare go into a square church because I'm afraid God will trap me in a corner and hold me accountable for my past behavior."

The arteries in his legs continued to deteriorate. Despite hand wringing around him, my roommate remained jovial. He told his family not to fret. "If the Lord wants me elsewhere, I'm ready. I know there's more to come in the next chapter of my life."

In contrast, my situation was improving. I expected to be discharged in a few days. Still, I was glum. My professional life involved long and often hectic hours. My illness was an enforced break but I couldn't forget the work piling up at the office. My thoughts were so filled with problems the idea I might experience joy at the hospital seemed only a dream. Seriousness was my life. Seeing my state, my roommate took me to task.

"You can't avoid unpleasantness," he said. "Unexpected, unhappy events happen every day. But letting them get to you is silly. Do that, and you'll never have inner peace. You've got to learn to live with negative people and things. You counteract it by pausing now and then to see and recognize the joy trying to reach you. It may just be a thought, a smile from a colleague or a vision of the good you're doing. Whatever it is, joy is always as close as the next moment. Pause the daily nonsense every now and you'll soon see it."

Thankfully, my roommate's hospital stay had a happy ending. For reasons that baffled his doctors, blood circulation spontaneously returned to his legs. Even the damage caused by the event was controllable with medication. Within two days he was released to spend more time enjoying life and spreading joy to others. I remained hospitalized a little longer.

As night settled on the day he left, I received a direct dial-in phone call hours after phones to patient rooms were supposedly shut down. A familiar voice said, "I thought you might be missing me. Things were so busy when I left I forgot to tell you something.

I see a good man who's letting little things get him down. Start relaxing your way through problems. Take a moment to look for the joy. It's there. Put the problem and joy together and you'll amaze yourself with the result. If you need a reminder, think of me enjoying putting tires on cars. Now have a restful night and a great tomorrow."

I'd heard of angels but it wasn't until that moment I realized I'd been living and talking to one all week.

CHAPTER 21

Got White Coat Syndrome? Try This

Visiting a doctor is a slightly traumatic experience for me. I get nervous walking in the outer office door. It's not that my doctor is impersonal. He's very approachable. My nervousness stems from the irrational fear I might receive an unfavorable diagnosis or be embarrassed because I didn't follow past instructions to take better care of myself. My feelings may be silly but they are real and they at times have unfortunate physical and mental side effects.

I've tried slow breathing to calm down and lower my blood pressure when the office assistant comes to get a reading but that's been only modestly successful. I reluctantly conclude I am a victim of what is known as white coat syndrome. The white coat reference of course is to the fact many doctors wear white lab coats when working with patients. If white coat syndrome sounds eerily familiar, I'm happy to report I've found there are ways to deal with it.

Start by admitting you have the problem. Next remember in and of itself it's not serious. This is not to say you should ignore it. Some more serious problems share similar symptoms. Tell your doctor about these feelings and let him or her determine your situation.

Symptoms associated with white coat syndrome include nervousness, elevated blood pressure and reluctance to tell a doctor important information when in the office. I know an elderly individual who is notorious for this. His standard reply when a doctor asks about his health is "Great!" In reality he has trouble eating, is losing weight, doesn't sleep well and regularly experiences a variety of recurring aches and pains. Fortunately, his doctor knows him well. After asking how he's doing and getting the "great!" response he turns to the family member accompanying him for the "real" information.

People afflicted with white coat syndrome deal with the problem in variety of ways. Some avoid seeing a doctor unless they feel their situation is critical. Some use ideas and suggestions from actors portraying doctors in TV series and in pharmaceutical ads to avoid a real doctor. This is dangerous. Only an examination by a licensed physician can determine if symptoms are serious or benign.

Just as worrisome are those who try to avoid doctor visits by using information obtained through Internet searches.

They self medicate with over the counter or alternative medicines. Sites like WebMD, the Mayo and Cleveland Clinics can be helpful when used correctly. But, they are not intended to replace a doctor's diagnosis and prescriptions. They exist to provide background information on illnesses identified by physicians. Trying to self-treat anything but a Band-Aid wound, simple headache or common cold is, at best, chancy.

Fortunately, if doctor visits make you uncomfortable, there are things you can do to ease the anxiety. They start with preparing for the appointment. Here are a few suggestions.

- Write up a list of the symptoms or concerns that are prompting the visit. Be as specific as possible.

- Prepare a list of questions you would like to discuss with the doctor.

- Carry a list of your current medications with you. Include all prescription and non-prescription medications and supplements you take regularly. Include dosages and times when you take them.

- Carry a list of all of the doctors you see (include eye doctors and dentists). Include their office phone numbers and addresses. Also include the name and phone number of your preferred pharmacy.

- Carry a copy of your medical history. Your doctor probably has this information on file but it might be helpful if a question about a past event arises.

- Carry a small pad of paper and use it to jot down your doctor's comments and instructions so you don't forget them when you get home.

If you're extremely nervous about a doctor visit, consider taking a companion with you. A family member or close friend can ease your waiting room anxiety and, if your modesty can handle it and the doctor approves, accompany you into the examining room.

White coat syndrome is understandable. Your health is at stake and it is right to be concerned. However, try not to permit an ache or pain to go from a minor nuisance to a catastrophe in your mind. Likewise don't avoid a doctor because you suffer from this syndrome.

Prepare for the visit as suggested and keep in mind your doctor is on your side. He or she wants you to be healthy and stay that way. Let the doctor do his or her job. Think also of the peace of mind you'll gain from the visit. If you need treatment, you'll be on your way to health. If you're already healthy, you'll know and appreciate this fact. Sounds like a win-win doesn't it.

CHAPTER 22

Bored?

Boredom is the mind's way of telling us to extend ourselves. If we don't have something outside us to think about and work on, our mind may start working on our bodies leading to illness. TV watching, reading a book or newspaper or socializing on the Internet helps but sitting and viewing is not doing. It's input without output. We are born to think AND do.

Studies indicate activity not only keeps our minds busy, it has real physical benefits. It can lower our cholesterol risk, type-two diabetes, and blood pressure to name a few. It also improves our energy and mood by negating depression. Boredom is an internal problem only we can correct. The cure starts with setting achievable goals. Being one of the first people to land on Mars may seem like a great goal but is it achievable for you in your lifetime? Focus on real possibilities not fantasies. Once you've set goals, get up and get moving. Activities don't have to be earthshaking but they must take us outside our heads.

On my ninth birthday I received a postage stamp album and a bag full of stamps from nations around the world. Stamps didn't sound as exciting as baseball and football with friends so I ignored them for a long time. Months later, I found myself with nothing to do on a rainy Saturday. I noticed the stamps and album on my bookshelf so I pulled them out and began a new phase of my life.

Amazed at holding real items from countries around the world, I grabbed an atlas and found the source of each stamp. I couldn't believe how far they'd traveled to get to me. My school geography class suddenly became interesting. When we studied a place, I pictured my stamp from that country and instantly felt a connection to its people. By the time I was fifteen, I was determined to visit as many of these countries as I could. I even made a list of places I intended to go.

It's been 60 years since I created that list and I'm happy to report I've been to over 60 of the countries on six of the seven continents. Antarctica is the exception but I won't rule out a future trip. As for the U.S., I've only missed Rhode Island and Arkansas. I don't know why, but I'm sure I'll get to them.

I chose travel as my number one goal because it's interesting and fairly easy to do. Anticipating a trip, planning it, taking it and remembering it keeps my mind active. If world travel is not necessarily appealing to you, keep in mind you can also travel close to home. Pick a place nearby that you've never visited. Go to a park, a museum, a historic site, an unusual business, or ethnic restaurant. Meet new people. I guarantee the experiences will alter the way you view your daily routine.

When I taught high school and was still single, I had several weeks off each summer. One year rather than sit around or take a part time job, I decided to make a solo car trip around the western US and Canada. I had no itinerary. I just got in the car and went west, changing direction when I heard about something interesting.

I crossed the Canadian plains, attended the famous Stampede rodeo in Calgary, Alberta, visited the Canadian Rockies and the city of Vancouver. I turned south to Seattle, Washington, Portland, Oregon and the magnificent Oregon coast. I visited California's Redwoods, the Golden Gate city of San Francisco then Los Angeles. Using my old broadcasting credentials I even wangled a VIP tour of the MGM movie studios. Wow! I met and had lunch with movie stars in the studio commissary and watched scenes from two different movies being filmed. All it took to get in was the boldness to ask and do.

My return trip took me to many of the great cities and national parks of Nevada, Arizona, New Mexico, Utah and Colorado. Operating on a tight budget, I stayed in small mom and pop budget motels, bought my food at grocery stores and enjoyed lunches and dinners at picnic tables in scenic spots. The trip was one continuous series of priceless experiences.

It might sound lonely to travel on your own but it's not. Loneliness is a decision and I decided to have none of it. When I arrived at a big city, I took a sight seeing bus tour. This guaranteed I'd see and visit the city's major points of interest and allowed me to meet other travelers with whom I often had lunch or dinner. When on my own, I'd ask service station attendants, store clerks and others to suggest things I should see and do. Their responses took me to fabulous out of the way spots known mainly to locals. I even drove the highest paved automobile road in North America (Mt. Evens, Colorado). It was wonderfully scary as I worked my way to the top at 14,265 feet. Light-headedness from altitude, made the descent on the outside lane with no guardrails and thousand foot drops interesting. I'm sure my prayers didn't hurt, but what an experience! Days driving alone gave me time to reflect on what I'd done and plan where to go next. The trip took several weeks and covered miles and miles of our wonderful country. Memories created along the way are still bright places in my thoughts.

If a large trip is too extravagant or time consuming, take day trips instead. Use your home as your hotel and restaurant. Get a local guidebook or go on-line and find those special treasures around you. I learned we have John King Books, a fabulous used bookstore in Detroit. Located in a historic multistory warehouse King's has historic books on almost every subject imaginable. I discovered even more about my city just talking to people I met there.

If you once played a musical instrument or sang, even if you haven't done so for a while, consider joining a community band, orchestra or choir. They'll help you get back into performance shape. Check with your city hall, school district or local newspaper to see if they can direct you.

Volunteer at a non-profit organization. Giving to others is a great way to kill boredom, bring good into your life and make new friends. Hospitals, nursing homes, charitable groups, city and school programs, recreation groups and more are always looking for people. Say... if you're a golfer, check with a local public golf course to see if they need help. Starter and ranger jobs may not be paid but free playing time is often included.

Do something frightening (when the fear is not unreasonable). Conquering a fear gives you an uplifting sense of accomplishment and may even open doors to new opportunities and excitements. Learn to swim. Ride a rollercoaster. Take a Toastmasters speaker training program. Go hiking on a wilderness trail (with a guide or at least a good guidebook). If auto racing appeals, check with a local racetrack to see about driving one of their cars or your own on their track. Many offer this program to adult licensed drivers with good driving records.

Do something you've never done. The mind craves novelty. Stretch a little by learning a craft, going fishing or joining a gym. Visit an art museum. Go camping. Walk in a parade. Many communities have them on holidays. Build a piece of furniture. Become a ham radio operator. Run a 5K marathon. Attend a symphony orchestra concert or a stage play. Go to a flea or farmers market.

Call or visit someone you haven't seen or heard from in a while. If they were once significant in your life, they helped make you who you are. Celebrate through a reconnection.

Smile at and strike up a brief conversation with a stranger. At best you may find a new friend or have a moment or two of connection that will lift your spirit. At worst, they'll ignore or reject you. Nothing ventured, nothing gained.

Do something you've always considered too wild. For example, consider taking a sample-flying lesson in a light plane. The cost is usually more affordable than you might imagine and the experience maximum. Check with a local general aviation airport for information. Consider a hot air balloon ride. You'll see your area from an entirely new perspective. Try scuba diving or snorkeling. There are hundreds of choices. Check newspapers and tourist guides for possibilities.

Most of all… remember life is to be lived not endured while waiting for something better. Why be bored? when getting into action will allow you to live the adventurous life others envy?

CHAPTER 23

Dealing with Stress

The fun loving character I'd known since college suddenly turned into a weary grouch. At the insistence of his wife he had a physical exam. The results indicated no dread diseases but did suggest he was suffering from a potential body damaging condition called stress.

A successful business executive, my seemingly comfortable with himself friend was now withdrawn, fidgety and irritable. I joined him on his backyard deck one Saturday afternoon and following general chitchat asked what was going on.

He told me the long time beloved CEO at his workplace had retired and been replaced by a younger man. The new boss was smooth and well spoken in pubic but tyrannical toward employees. Unlike his predecessor who built the company on teamwork, the new boss seemed to have only two concerns – generating revenue and personally looking good to company board members and the public.

Those who worked with him directly, including my friend, quickly discovered the new CEO had limited planning, management and people skills. He was insensitive, insecure and insincere. He viewed company executives as potential rivals to be neutralized. He saw employees as replaceable cogs. If they requested improvements in salary, benefits or working conditions he wanted them replaced. He trusted no one. His off the top of his head management style was typified by constant changes in program direction and invented crises he felt would make him look like a hero saving the company from disaster. The impact on my friend was non-stop stress and his health was beginning to suffer.

A look at the global business climate reveals my friend's situation is not unique. Business and health publications regularly carry stories that say the effects of stress are one of the world's great health concerns. Millions of lost work hours annually are attributed to stress related illness.

The Internet based health information service *Health Line* recently revealed why stress is so hurtful. It seems stress activates the body's ancient flight or fight protective response mechanism. This mechanism was an essential life preserver for thousands of years when life was more physically oriented. With notable exceptions (i.e. war zones), the flight or fight response for most people is today less critical. Nonetheless, even modest stress can have a serious negative impact on body systems.

Apparently when our mind senses stress it directs the release of cortisol and adrenaline stored in various glands into the rest of the body. These chemicals tense muscles and activate our immune system to make us ready for physical threat or injury. Once released however, these hormones do not quickly disburse even when the danger does not materialize or the fear passes. They flow through the body for some time and can cause harm by mistaking normal tissue for an invader.

A body in stress also diverts oxygen from the brain to muscles making them ready to repel attack. This hampers our thinking and reasoning abilities. The result is a reduction in our creative and intuitive thinking. Faced with diminished brain direction, our body's instinctual nature takes command. Any inclination toward finding a peaceful alternative in a situation is thus reduced.

This stress reaction causes blood vessels to constrict raising blood pressure forcing the heart to work harder. Hypertension and blood vessel disorders are common side effects.

Under stress, our liver produces extra blood sugar to provide muscles with bursts of energy. Unfortunately, it does not shut down quickly following a threat. Long after a crisis has passed, excess sugar remains in body systems stressing sugar regulating systems and over time can lead to type-two diabetes.

Hours after a severe stress response, our energy-depleted body may show signs of exhaustion. If the stress – response cycle is repeated frequently our bodies may become deficient in vitamins and minerals leading to malnutrition, obesity, and cardiovascular problems.

Health Line reports five or more years of untreated stress can result in rheumatoid arthritis, gastro intestinal illnesses such as Crohn's disease or systemic illnesses like Lupus. According to the *National Institute of Mental Health*, people under chronic stress are susceptible to viral infections like the flu and common cold and are less likely to benefit from vaccines such as the flu shot.

Helping my friend understand the effects of stress was useful but what he really needed was an immediate plan for dealing with it. *The Cleveland Clinic's Center for Integrative Medicine's* on-line site provided suggestions.

Cleveland staff said a quick and temporary way to reduce stress is to use a simple breathing technique. At the start of a stress episode, breathe slowly and deeply ten times focusing only on breathing. This act apparently delays triggering of the body's basic stress response long enough to give the brain an opportunity to decide if there is a better way to cope with the problem.

Frequent stress episodes require additional action. *The Physicians Committee for Responsible Medicine* suggests a shift in foods can help. They recommend including high-fiber carbohydrate-rich foods, fruits and vegetables in our diet. They also recommend limiting high-fat foods, caffeine, and sugar in all forms including alcohol (it is essentially liquid sugar). Sugar stimulates excessive production of the hormone insulin that has the same negative effect as stress hormones.

The Physicians Committee also recommends a physical workout three times a week to balance the thyroid gland and keep the body needing fewer hormones to prepare for a flight or fight response. They note marshal arts programs such as Kung Fu or Taekwondo are helpful because of their total body building exercises.

Our fast paced, computer driven, sensational news reporting and multinational business climate is a perfect medium for stress. Fortunately, we don't have to be a victim. Even small changes in thinking and behavior can make a huge difference in our response to it.

My friend eased himself into these techniques and over time took control of his stress. In the end he went farther. He determined he didn't need his present job. He looked for options and before long was working at a new company, still in his home area, with similar compensation and a much more relaxed environment. He took control and became the hero rather than victim in his stress story.

CHAPTER 24

Are Memories Clouding Your Future?

Recalling the past helps us make decisions about today's events and tomorrow's possibilities. They remind us of the effort our ancestors made to improve life quality. They remind us how far man has progressed from prehistory to modern times. Memories should be savored, but not made into guidelines for future action.

Emphasis on memories can lead to overlooking and glorifying past realities. Memories are tainted with emotion. They can, for example, deceive us into thinking the past was a simpler easier time with higher moral values. Nothing could be further from the truth.

Dr. Otto Bettmann, founder of New York's famed Bettmann Archive, a resource that includes millions of historic photos, films and literature became concerned when he observed people trying to deal with today's challenges by clinging to inaccurate notions of the past.

In his book titled, *The Good Old Days, They Were Terrible!*, Bettmann sought to remind readers of the danger in memories. Focusing on America, Bettmann observed the period from the nation's founding to the mid twentieth century was far less golden than Hollywood movies might lead us to believe. While some wealthy people lived lavishly, the average American worked ten to twelve hour days six to seven days a week for or slightly above subsistence wages. Child labor was common as families needed to generate all of the income they could to acquire food and shelter. There was little or no government regulation of business. Foods and medicines were therefore often contaminated for profit (i.e. sawdust added to flour to make it go farther was typical).

Smoke & gasses pollution from business and home coal and wood burning furnaces and appliances made air quality unhealthy. Sanitation systems were primitive or non-existent. Water was often contaminated by sewage as leaky water and sewer lines converged. Illness was common. Medical services were fundamental. Diseases were widespread and cures as yet unknown. Alcoholism was prevalent as people chose to drink germ-killing alcohol infused beverages rather than contaminated water or to try to block out daily hardships. Working conditions and housing for all but a few was crowded and dirty. The life span of working people was short and misery a constant companion. Nonviolent and violent crime in cities was so extensive, gentleman of means found it necessary to carry a cane containing a sword or a small pocket pistol to protect themselves.

Bettman emphasized making a better future requires openness to new ideas, ideals, tools and techniques and a realistic understanding of the past. Memories are fun in museums, at re-enactor events and holiday parades but not as guide to the future.

Our thoughts, family albums and saved treasures keep us aware of where we've been. They help us appreciate the contributions of our forebears. But, memories are far too subject to emotion to be the primary guide to present and future activities. Consider them in future planning but rely more heavily on present experiences and future projections when charting a forward course .

As Bettmann points out, applying past notions, rules and regulations to the present will lead to perpetuation of past problems. Only by evaluating the past in terms of today's circumstances, needs and desires can we position ourselves to take advantage of the good still to arrive.

CHAPTER 25

Why Change?

I have a friend who bristles whenever someone suggests he change his habits. He's anti computers, smart phones and what he calls unnecessary gadgets. "I'm not about to chase after every new thing that comes along," he says. "It's not that I'm anti everything new. I just need a darn good reason to alter my well-established routine."

When I heard he subscribed to cable TV I teased him about his anti new attitude. His response was logical. "My favorite sports are now only on cable." He didn't add an Internet connection saying, "I've heard of email and tweety something but I don't need it."

My friend prefers his news on paper and movies in theaters. He drives a large car rather than a small fuel-efficient model because, he says, it's comfortable. He is personable, generous and engaging. He's also unwilling to concede the world he entered three quarters of a century ago is rapidly receding into old photographs, movies, museums and history books.

He did surprise us a few months ago when he showed up at a meeting with a cell phone. It was an old style flip up unit but apparently served his purpose. "My new boss told me I needed one," he said. "It's a part time on call job so they keep in touch with us contractors through messages. Actually, I find it handy now that pay phones are almost impossible to find. I also use it to keep in touch with friends and family."

The twenty-first century is awash in technology inspired change. Post office staff struggle to remain viable as much first class mail is diverted to electronic delivery. News and information, once only available in paper newspapers and magazines, is now available in electronic form for instant delivery over the Internet. Manufacturing is decentralized with much going to less costly third world nations. At home, industry automation grows. A plant owner recently told me his milling machine staff once consisted of eighteen people working over three shifts. It is now down to three. With automation, a single operator can control up to six machines simultaneously.

The financial industry is changing. We can now receive and pay bills, make bank deposits, get cash (ATM machines) and arrange loans on-line. In Boston a while back, I walked into a bank expecting to see tellers. They were gone! All stations were ATMs (automatic teller machines). There was only one woman at a desk at the end of the room. When I explained I was unsure how to use these machines, she smiled and said, "That's why I'm here. I help people like you get started with our new system." Even transportation is affected. New air and ground systems permit us to physically travel nearly anywhere in the world within a 24 hour span.

Rapidly developing technology is sparking uncertainty, confusion, opposition and turmoil among people around the globe. A large Canadian bank seeing what was happening once highlighted the problem in a customer newsletter. They likened the effect of today's changes to playing a baseball game where the bases are moveable. As soon as a ball is hit, defending players can pick up the base bags and move them anywhere they choose in fair territory. The batter never knows in advance where he must run to be safe. Quelling the stress accompanying change requires learning to deal with it. The task begins by accepting the fact we will change as the society around us does. Change is inevitable.

Not sure this is true? Look around you. Change is a constant. In nature, storms, floods, earthquakes, forest fires, mudslides, avalanches, climate alterations and more regularly alter the Earth. In the heavens, astronomers watch as stars and planet are born and die. Comets, space storms, meteors and more regularly impact the things they pass. Discoveries and inventions from prehistoric tools to electricity, the telephone, automobiles, airplanes, radio, TV, antibiotics and X rays have and will continue to change living conditions for humans. Hanging on to the past may be good for museum professionals but for most of us it's not realistic. Our world demands we find useful approaches for dealing with new and old alike.

The place to start is by reserving judgment on something new until we understand its advantages and disadvantages. Many horse drawn wagon manufacturers of the late 19th century dismissed the automobile as a noisy impractical contraption. In less than 20 years, the majority of these companies were out of business. Flexible ones, like the Studebaker brothers of South Bend Indiana, embraced the automobile. They added engines to their wagon bodies then continuously improved the marriage. Studebaker was profitable well into the second half of the 20th century when newly merged competitors drove them out of business with innovative and less expensive ways to build cars.

While change is pervasive, it is unwise to embrace it before understanding its positives and negatives. Waiting too long however can also be risky. Perhaps the best idea is to approach change like a seasoned gambler. Know the odds and move only when they seem favorable.

The old saying, "What you don't know can't hurt you," does not apply to change. Those seeking personal and professional success in the age of change must find time to monitor what's happening by scanning trade and trend magazines, financial movements and economic potentials on a regular basis.

I once participated in a weeklong seminar on product forecasting. The group consisted of 34 executives from major corporations and me, an interested educator. During the week we learned to analyze product capabilities, market potential and other key factors necessary for success. At the end of the week we were divided into teams and given information on real products currently under development by major corporations.

We were tasked with assessing each product's viability and potential for economic success. We did the work and wrote our reports. During the following year, each product was introduced. At the end of that year we each received packets containing copies of our reports, predictions and the success or failure of each item.

In each case, our predictions proved to be correct. One of the companies ignored our analysis. They, unfortunately, are no longer in business. Dealing with change does not require the in-depth work we did but without some advance study and analysis of a change, the odds of success are likely to be no better than those of lottery ticket purchasers.

My friend, tries to avoid change and he gets away with it most of the time because he is happily retired with relatively simple needs and desires. Those who must still work for their living seldom have this luxury. Change is a constant. Those who learn to accept and live with it are the people most likely to experience future success.

CHAPTER 26

Is Your Life Out of Balance?

The 1995 movie *Sabrina* provides an example of someone living in balance. The heroine's father is the chauffer for a wealthy family. He lives on their estate in a comfortable well-appointed apartment over the garage. He drives family members and guests as needed leaving him considerable personal time. He is social but prefers to spend much of his free time reading and writing. He has a good income, excellent benefits, a comfortable place to live and a healthy investment portfolio. He has no desire to impress, dress for success (he wears a uniform while working) or scramble to achieve more. He is content.

Sabrina's father knows what he wants, acts appropriately and attracts good. We too can achieve his state of contentment if we're willing to understand and employ the principle that directs his life.

It's called balance and it's the key to comfortable living. It affects all aspects of life. Once we know what to look for we see it operating everywhere including nature, religion, science, art and more. Science refers to the principle as Newton's Third Law of Physics. Postulated by eighteenth century English scientist Sir Isaac Newton, the law says, "For every action there is an opposite and equal reaction." In other words, everything that happens is eventually balanced by its opposite.

In nature we find if we cut down trees on a forested slope, the reaction will be the erosion of the slope. It is stable only when tree roots hold its soil in place. Without them, it is subject to being washed away by rains and wind. Trees and earth form a balanced partnership. The trees only thrive and grow when the soil provides nutrients and rain the moisture needed to grow.

Balance goes beyond trees and slopes. Animals including humans exist in part because trees provide the oxygen needed for us to breathe. Oxygen also mixes with hydrogen to produce rain. Animals give off carbon dioxide which trees and plants require to flourish. Our eco system is a good example of the give and take (balance) necessary for things to thrive on this planet.

Our lives also require balance to flourish. If we wish to be healthy, we must balance work with play, food types and amounts, physical effort and rest, income and expenses and so on. The point is whatever we do or think, natural factors will attempt to balance it with other elements. If we try to force things to go only one way, we invite chaos and disease.

I once had an employee who had no understanding of the balance principle. She wanted luxurious living. To that end, she purchased and furnished a grand home. She leased an expensive car, took lavish vacations and wore expensive clothes. She had what she wanted but her life was anything but peaceful. Her modest salary was not compatible with her chosen lifestyle. She fought daily battles with creditors, experienced cash crunches and calls from people threatening to repossess all aspects of her dream life. Desperate, she asked me for advice.

Hearing her situation, I suggested she was living out of balance. I proposed two alternatives to help her regain it. First, she could sell off possessions, pay her bills and adopt a lifestyle in keeping with her income. Second, she could develop new skills and go after a higher paying job that would enable her to live the life she wanted. Her response surprised me. "Those are things a mature person would do," she said. "I don't want to change and I don't want to train for and get a new job." She then secretly chose alternative three.

She started missing work, supposedly due to illness. We later discovered she used time away from our office to earn extra income at another job. It and her sick pay allowed her to temporarily keep things together. It didn't take long for our insurance company to discover her fraudulent behavior however. Their findings led to her dismissal from both jobs. I later heard she lost her home, car, other items and her husband. Her life was mess. She thought she was too smart to have to follow the balance principle and lost.

Balancing lives is natural not difficult. It merely requires deciding the type of life we want (luxurious, adventurous, rustic, secure, free spirited, etc.). It requires we be specific about the nature of work we desire, the types of people we want around us and the things we want to possess. Once all aspects are identified, it's time to consider what we're willing to do to balance our wants with the energy and effort required to get and keep them.

Among other things find out what knowledge, licenses, experience and other elements are needed. Identify the time and resources we will need. Armed with the appropriate information, make a decision. What are we willing to give to get what we want? This is the point where fantasy and reality separate. The balance principle requires giving to receive. Miss on either point and you may end up unhappy.

Complicating a balance plan, is the fact that even when preparation is done and we are hard at work, life may throw in a surprise. Illness, natural disasters, economic reversals, accidents and more may affect a balance plan. Here is where learning the value of flexibility comes in handy.

One of my daughters took a job with a Fortune 500 company following graduation from college. A few years later she found the work she trained for to be less absorbing and attractive than she had imagined. She wanted more out of life. She needed to rebalance so she explored alternatives by volunteering during off work hours at local nonprofit groups. She fell in love with all aspects of the work at a local history museum. She then decided to enroll in night history classes at a local university. Over time she earned a second degree in history and a graduate degree in museum studies. She left her business employer and is now happily working at a major museum. She rebalanced and moved on by giving then getting her dream work.

Signs our lives are out of balance include frequent illness, dissatisfaction with what we're doing, weight gain, physical exhaustion and feelings of negative self worth. Each signal suggests it is time to review life circumstances.

Begin with an objective look at what we're doing. Is our giving and getting in the proper proportions to balance each other? As we mature, it is not unusual to take on added responsibilities. This can lead to work loads so great we have little time to maintain balance between work and play. Untended, this situation can lead to burnout.

If we find depression and illness becoming constant companions, it's time for adjustments. When work time cannot be easily adjusted, we must find ways to include play in it. Mild office pranks, contests, conversations and staff activities can lighten work life. If the workload is so heavy it cannot accommodate play, it may time to look for other work. Review your desires and plans, add information on alternative options and see where it takes you. It may be a new job, location, relationship or other element is in your future so you can regain balance.

In the meantime, make non-work time as enjoyable as possible. Limit "downer" movies, TV talk shows and newscasts. Get into fun activities such as community sports, interest groups, dinners with friends and family, and an intriguing hobby or just hang out with people who make you feel good about yourself. Who knows? These activities may be all you need to get back into balance.

Always remember nature abhors imbalance. We can only be at our best when our lives are in balance. Time spent achieving this state is always time well spent.

CHAPTER 27

Often Sick? Consider This

Occasional colds, flu, or upset stomachs are normal but a lingering illnesses needs attention. A doctor can determine the true nature of an illness and select appropriate treatment. If no serious illness is detected yet we continue to feel ill, things may get complicated. It may mean it's time to examine more than our immediate health. It may be time to look at the way we are living.

The term lifestyle illness is being increasingly applied to sicknesses that can be helped or avoided with changes in our behavior. Dr. Mladen Golubic, medical director of the Center for Lifestyle Medicine at the Cleveland Clinic, suggests lifestyle choices such as smoking, alcohol abuse, inadequate diet, lack of physical activity and failure to adopt effective ways for reducing stress are leading factors in chronic diseases such as obesity, type 2 diabetes, hypertension, cardiovascular disease and several types of cancer.

Dr. Golubic's words came to mind while doing my chaplain rounds. I met a man hospitalized with shortness of breath and chest pain. He was restless, weak and discouraged. I introduced myself and asked about his ailments. His answer was direct. "I'm here hoping my doctor can cure or at least slow the effects of my stupidity before they kill me."

He told me he was a combat toughened Marine who spent years internalizing habits that now are impacting his health. "As a Marine," he said, "I always out lifted, out carried and out fought everyone in my unit." When I left the Corps, I took a construction job where I easily handled tasks others found back breaking. I went years thinking I was as close to invincible as a human can get. Then my habits caught up with me. I'd started smoking at thirteen and eventually worked my way to two and a half packs a day. A few years ago, shortness of breath sent me to the emergency room. Tests showed I have COPD (chronic obstructive pulmonary disorder) linked to smoking. My doctor got things under control but a few months later, a heart irregularity appeared. Looking at my history and recent tests, he said years of beer soaked happy hours and greasy foods together with my smoking seem to have taken a toll on my heart. I realized at the rate I'm going I could end up with a little of everything you guys treat around here."

The man was not unique. Despite publicity on the dangers

of poor health habits, many of us continue to engage in illness generating behaviors. A 1994 study repeated in 2005 by researchers at the University of Alberta, Canada attempted to discover why people don't change habits when they know they cause health problems. The answers in both studies were practically identical. Leading the list of reasons was a desire for social acceptance. Close behind was "to relieve stress." Others suggested advertising makes these activities seem fun and harmless. Few said they considered any long-term negative effects from their actions.

Anyone uncertain about the effect some of their behaviors may have on their health ought to take a few moments to think about them. Smoking several cigarettes or other tobacco products daily, drinking more than an occasional alcoholic beverage, overeating, avoiding exercise, getting too little sleep and participating in contact sports or extreme physical challenges all have known long term negative effects on the human body.

Frequent illnesses may be a sign trouble is brewing in our bodies. Only a doctor can determine if a problem is physical, psychological or lifestyle. If the examination indicates lifestyle, the cure may be almost totally in our hands. On the positive side, a lifestyle illness does not have to be a curse. It can be the key that moves us to changes that will reinvigorate and extend our lives.

Deciding to change a habit is a starting point. The task is

usually not as simple as it sounds. Undoing something we've done a long time may take special effort.

Change starts with understanding why we adopted a habit in the first place. It may be surprising to find out, as in the case of overeating, the reason began in childhood. Do you remember the "clean plate club" or mom and dad using sweets as a reward when we were good or upset? Many of us have kept these traditions. Other reasons include, "I just drink to relax and release stress after a tough day (at work, with family, etc.)." Whatever the reasons, if it's time to change, we must deal with them. The task requires thinking through causes and solutions.

Grab a sheet of paper and a pen or a pencil and spend a few minutes thinking about your situation. Draw two lines down the sheet to make three columns. Title the columns left to right" Habits, Excuses, and Feelings. Now, write under Habits things you do that you believe or your doctor suggests are injurious to your health. Under Excuses, write reasons you use to justify why you do each activity (i.e. stress, celebration, down, loneliness, etc.). Under Feelings, write how you feel when you engage in the habit (e.g. I feel good/ bad when I _____.

When your paper is complete, review what you've said about yourself. You may become aware (perhaps for the first time) how your emotions trigger your unhealthy habits. Use this information to consider health-oriented changes you need to make (i.e. stop skipping breakfast, get more sleep, drink alcohol only on special occasions, give up cigarettes).

If you seem to have a lifestyle problem, don't rely on will power to handle it. Get support. Tell your doctor about your intentions and heed his or her advice. Consider joining a weight control, substance abuse or general counseling program. Local churches, hospitals, libraries, public and private services and organizations are good sources for finding these groups.

If you are spiritual, consider meditation. Meditation is quieting the mind in an attempt to achieve a sense of oneness with the universal power. It can add a sense of peace and strength to help you achieve your goal.

Neuroscientists at the University of Pennsylvania report brain scans of people during meditation show definite changes from their non-meditating state. If you're unfamiliar with meditation yet wonder if it might help you conquer a negative habit, seek information and support through your doctor, minister, priest or health center.

CHAPTER 28

Seeing is Believing?

There was a time when we thought a picture might be worth a thousand words. Perhaps that is still true but it doesn't guarantee what we see or read is true. Changes in communications media have created a world where just about anything presented in any form can be manipulated to make falsehoods look true and truth look false.

Visuals have long been manipulated to suit the storytelling needs of moviemakers. The skills and hardware needed however were difficult to get and very expensive. This limit confined their use to major film studios. But things have changed. Today the computer has made media manipulation so easy and inexpensive practically anyone with inexpensive equipment can do it. This brings into question the validity of what we see, hear or read.

I once did a unit on this subject with a group of high school students. The manipulated media trend was just gaining momentum. To get discussion going I shared a then popular television commercial loaned to me by a friend involved in its production.

The commercial showed attractive young people playing music, engaged in sports and picnicking on a sunny beach. One look and you wanted to be part of what they were doing. The sponsor's intent was to convince viewers that drinking its soft drink would get them included in similar activities in their own area. There was only one problem. Little of what was shown was real. Using outtake footage also supplied by my friend, I allowed my students to see the difference between video fantasy and reality.

The beach crowds were actors selected for their physical attractiveness. Those whose bodies included blemishes, wrinkles, too much weight or lacked a good tan had these problems "corrected" with special video altering tools. Even the sky was not immune to correction. It was made bluer and contained puffier clouds than nature provides. Ocean waves were enhanced to make them appear ideal for surfing. Beach sand was made whiter and cleaner than found in nature. My students were shocked as I pointed out one video manipulation after another.

Altering reality is common in today's advertising, movies, television and news. Producers want to make their stories, messages and stars as appealing as possible. The effect on viewers, in addition to encouraging the purchase of products and programs, is to distort notions of what's real and what is not. If you've ever been unhappy with your image in a mirror because it doesn't look like people you see on TV and movie screens, stop! Most of them don't look like that either. What you see on screen are carefully manipulated images.

I witnessed media magic first hand at a Detroit production studio during my broadcast days. On a break from doing commercial narrations, I explored other studios. In a photo studio, I met a woman working with food. She said she was a food dresser and invited me to watch her make food look irresistible in photos for print ads, on menus and restaurant posters.

At one point, she took a raw frozen hamburger patty and quickly seared its outside so it looked cooked. The middle of the patty remained frozen. She then burned lines on the surface of the patty with a curling iron so it would look like it just came off a grill. A spray of a water/glycerin solution made the patty look juicy. Carefully placing the patty on a puffy semi-frozen bun she added semi-frozen lettuce and tomatoes. Another spray of the water/glycerin solution added to the fresh look. She added dashes of red and yellow acrylic paints made to look like ketchup and mustard, placed a semi frozen pickle slice next to the "burger" and sprayed the whole creation with a little hairspray to keep things in place. Her masterpiece complete, the burger was ready for the camera. I then knew why the resulting mouth watering photo looked nothing like the squished greasy burgers I get at my local fast food restaurant.

Burger complete, the woman introduced more eye pleasing tricks. She used mashed potatoes to represent ice cream because, she said, "it doesn't melt giving the photographer more time to get his shots." She made French fries appealing by keeping them frozen then spraying on a thin coat of yellow/tan dye and sprinkling them with vegetable oil and salt mix. Today, food dressers do much of this work with computers saving time and money.

Making the unreal look real is not limited to advertisers and moviemakers. With a computer and inexpensive software anyone with practice can distort photo reality. Did your neighbor really climb Mt. Everest? Did the woman down the street really get special permission to sit in the front row at a White House press conference?

The CEO of a company I once worked for came up with what he thought would be a staff morale booster. It was summer's end and everybody was back from vacations. So we could all share our exploits, he encouraged employees to post a few vacation photos on a large staff bulletin board. To make the project interesting, he even offered a free lunch to staff in the department that had the most people in exotic places.

A talented company photographer saw the contest as a personal challenge. He collected photos of famous places around the world from on-line sources. He took photos of staff posed so he could fit them into the exotic photos.

Using his computer and photo modification software, he produced photos of staff members riding rickshaws in Beijing, driving past the pyramids in Egypt, scuba diving on Australia's Great Barrier Reef, on safari in Africa, visiting sites in India and climbing the Alps in Europe.

The photos were remarkable. His department easily won the contest. When staff in other departments cried foul, the photographer owned up to what he'd done. The CEO was so delighted with the excitement generated by the project he had a lunch catered for all staff. Everyone had a good laugh and a good lunch. We also walked away with a new understanding of how easy it is to make the unreal look real.

As much fun as media manipulation can be when used for innocent pranks, it also has a not so nice side. It can be difficult to detect truth from falsehood. It is possible to put words into someone's mouth using even home equipment. Some Internet social media users subject viewers to distorted and false material that looks incredibly real. Protecting ourselves from misinformation has become a task we must all undertake. If we are to limit false judgments we must become media cynics. This applies to entertainment programs, advertising and even news reports all of whom reap financial rewards by securing large numbers of viewers.

Television news media use multiple tricks to attract viewers. To make a news story appear more significant than it is, they gather a small group of people together, move the camera in until the group fills the screen then suggest a mob was present at the event.

News "teasers" are another favorite. A "teaser" is a short audio or video segment that airs like ads during entertainment programs. The teaser promotes what appears to be a high interest story that will be included in the station's next newscast. Teasers may show video of tearful or injured people, police cars, fire trucks, ambulances, the outside of hospitals, courthouses, schools or legislative buildings. They are often augmented by an off camera deep voiced semi breathless announcer who suggests we will be shocked, frightened, angry or otherwise emotional about whatever they're trying to get viewers to watch. Of course the station will not tell us more until their nightly newscast. In most instances the actual "news" is not nearly as dire, exciting or big as the "teaser" suggests.

At the 2017 Academy Awards program a short segment showed how the media magicians took the image of an actor that had been dead for several years and made it appear he was alive and saying lines in a new movie. When media can resurrect the dead (figuratively) it's not hard to imagine unscrupulous individuals putting words in the mouths of politicians and other officials to defame them.

It is now up to us to protect ourselves from false and distorted information. A place to start is to consider most of what you see manipulated. Second, when you're really concerned, check what is said and done through reliable information fact checkers such as Snopes on the Internet before accepting information as valid.

There was a time when we had news gatekeepers such as broadcast networks, and major metropolitan newspapers to help us detect false news and information put out for public consumption. This role has changed dramatically over the past thirty years.

In 1949, the U.S. Federal Communications Commission (FCC) adopted a doctrine that required holders of broadcast licenses to present issues of public importance in a manner that was honest, equitable, and permitted all sides in a dispute equal access to the airwaves. This policy indirectly included broadcast networks because their programs aired on licensed stations.

In 1987, under pressure from political interests, the FCC formally removed this requirement. Relatively unregulated cable and Internet based "news" programs also entered the picture about this time. All of these reduced readership for newspapers and news magazines many of which have ceased publication.

It would not be inaccurate to say a political free-for-all now exists with news media. The old saying, "buyer beware" has never been truer. What we see, hear or read can no longer be accepted unless it is verified through a fact checking organization with a reputation for honesty and integrity.

Seeing is believing? Maybe yes and maybe no.

CHAPTER 29

Get Your Ideas Accepted

You have what you believe is a great idea but you need the help of others to make it happen. How do you go about getting support? As I searched for an answer, one name kept popping up - Thomas Edison. We remember him for his achievements in electric lighting, the phonograph, motion pictures and many other products. As important as these inventions became, I discovered they were the result not the cause of his success. Success came largely as a result of his ability to get people to listen to and buy into his ideas and inventions.

Edison's success can be traced to failure. In 1869 he patented the Electrographic Vote-Recorder. It was intended as a replacement for the often hours long roll call vote process in legislative bodies. Edson's machine could accurately do the job in minutes. What he didn't know however was legislators didn't want quick voting. They needed time for negotiating and arm-twisting. He never sold a single unit.

Years later Edison observed the vote recorder experience taught him a valuable lesson. He learned never to invent or introduce something for which he didn't know there was or for which he had not created, a market. His electric light was a prime example.

Edison did not invent electric illumination. That honor goes to British chemist Sir Humphrey Davey who in the early 1800's created the first electric light. Scientist more than an entrepreneur, Davey abandoned electric lighting when difficulties arose in making it practical. Others picked up the electric light mantle but also failed to produce a marketable product. Edison came along and applied dogged determination and marketing smarts learned from his first invention and ultimately change the world.

Edison's never-give-up spirit felt a suitable filament (the part of the light bulb that glows) could and would be found. He was so confident he assigned staff to experiment until they found one that worked. That task in motion, he was free to focus on making electric lighting marketable.

Up to and through most of the 19th century lighting consisted mainly of wood fires, candles, oil lamps and later natural gas burners. Each had drawbacks. They used open flames that had to be monitored for fire risk. Each emitted a smoky ashy residue that soiled rugs, draperies, upholstery and clothing and added to air pollution. They also produced fumes that required some windows be left ajar for ventilation. Gas lighting was brighter and more reliable than alternatives, but it still had too many open combustion drawbacks.

Preparing to answer the question why anyone would want electric illumination, Edison decided not to promote it as a new power and light source but rather "safe clean gas." Among his selling points were: electric light is not explosive, leaves no ash, can be left unattended for lengthy periods and requires no ventilation. He also noted he could bring it into homes and businesses using existing gas lighting pipes thus requiring minimal disturbance.

With promotion concepts in place, Edison turned to related needs. He would have to build electricity generating plants and distribution systems to get the power to homes and businesses. Doing this required gaining access to private and public property for poles and wires. Again using the gas company as a model, he requested right of way permissions from city officials using similar forms. City officials didn't see this as revolutionary. Edison was merely installing a desirable competitive safe gas.

Edison used familiar gas company terms and approaches thus his new "gas" did not generate mass concern. He was free therefore to focus on it's clear and desirable benefits.

Lasting and desirable changes seldom happen by accident. They require imagination, innovation, dedication and knowing how to get others on board. Edison provided a model. If we want to get ideas accepted, we can do little better than use Edison as an example. We can help people make a move we desire when we minimize their feelings of risk and discomfort.

CHAPTER 30

There is Always an Upside to Down

My paternal grandparents were show business people. They appeared in wild-west shows, circuses and on vaudeville stages during the late nineteenth and early twentieth centuries. Their comedy act included slack wire walking, lariat twirling and juggling. Passionate performers, they knew how to handle the ups and downs common to show business.

Every booking was subject to a last minute change. Trains carrying them from one performance site to another often arrived late. Disreputable theater owners, knowing it was too late for them to get another booking, would try to reduce performer wages upon their arrival. Performers needed flexibility and the grit to keep illness and hurts from showing during performances. I think of them often as I deal with unexpected events.

My grandparents' show business career spanned several decades. They loved performing and kept at it until changes in show business and the demands of a growing family forced them to reluctantly abandon the travel and economic uncertainty for a more settled life in one of the nation's then most thriving cities, Detroit.

My grandfather established a successful painting and decorating business and all went well until the Great Depression of the 1930's. My grandparents' bank like most of the era was caught without cash to pay depositors. It closed taking people's savings with them. Their nest egg was gone overnight. Jobs were lost. Unemployed people couldn't pay for goods and services. A small business, such as my grandfather's, was among the victims.

Just as things seemed at their darkest they got darker. The insurance company holding the mortgage on my grandparents' home called for an immediate and total payment of the balance. The company apologized but said they needed cash to pay off financial obligations. My grandparents had 30 days to pay or get out so their home could be seized and sold.

A lifetime as responsible hardworking people made no difference. Their seemingly secure world crumbled. With savings gone, their business destroyed and home taken, they found themselves broke and homeless with no immediate way to change things. They were down but then their show business character kicked in. They refused to be victims. They would find a way out of the mess and did.

They loaded their six-member family along with a few possessions into and on top of their old sedan and headed west looking for work and a place to live. My grandfather and father, a teen at the time, found work picking fruit in California. The meager income kept the family together until federally sponsored programs began to stimulate an economic recovery. It took time, but they survived and were eventually able to return to Michigan. My grandfather used his western savings to rent a home and reopen his painting and decorating business.

My grandparents viewed the Depression not unlike many challenges they experienced in show business. They set a goal to get back the life they'd lost. They were upset about the way their bank and mortgage company treated them but knew anger would do nothing to help them. The old stage slogan, "the show must go on," became their motto.

They focused on opportunities rather than misery. They spent money carefully and only returned to using banks after the creation of the Federal Deposit Insurance Corporation was established to protect depositor's money. They never fully trusted banks however. I didn't appreciate the depth of these feelings until after my father's death many years later. In going through his things I found twenty dollar bills rolled up in socks, underwear, jacket pockets, under liner paper, on dresser drawer bottoms and so on. He followed his family's tradition of making certain they always had emergency money in case banks again stripped them of their savings.

My grandfather died the day I was born so I never had the opportunity to meet him. Hanging around my grandmother however always included great amounts of laughter. She was a show business veteran. Sulking for any reason was not tolerated. The show (daily living) was the thing. Doing not just thinking was her idea of how to have a successful life.

My grandparents understood life, like a show business act, needed occasional refreshing. They were masters at adjusting. When wild-west shows, circuses and vaudeville had run their course, they took the cue and went into another line of work.

My father internalized this attitude. He graduated from law school when the Great Depression was in full swing. People struggling to find shelter and put food on the table couldn't afford a lawyer. The door to his profession was temporarily closed so he moved in another direction. A skilled musician, he saw big bands finding success with popular music. Scraping together a few dollars, he purchased a used clarinet and saxophone from a pawnshop. Teaching himself to play them, he was soon good enough to be hired by local jazz bands and eventually as a sideman in some of the big name traveling bands. A lawyer by day and musician by night, he used his musician income to pay family bills. Even after landing a secure law job in the 1940s, he continued to work music until 1950 when his day job made it necessary to move the family to another city.

Experience led him to pass an important notion along to me. I was working in radio right out of high school, loved it and expected to make a career in that business. My father didn't object but strongly suggested I balance what I was doing by developing at least one other paying skill. My grandparents' did this with show business and painting and decorating. My father did it with law and music. Both, through no fault of their own, found they needed the second occupation at a time in their lives.

Since going to college was popular when I graduated from high school, my dad encouraged me to get a degree. He didn't tell me what to study. He only wanted it to have job potential if I needed it. I attended college by day and worked as a disc jockey nights and weekends. I got a degree in the social sciences and a state certificate permitting me to teach. As fate would have it, my teaching degree ended up offering me better employment opportunities than broadcasting. I eventually became a teacher, administrator and college professor.

My family heritage accepted feeling down but only as a temporary condition. Their mantra was, "Brood for a short time if you must. But remember, life doesn't reward brooders. Success, joy and happiness come to those who do something with and about their circumstances."

Whether a problem is a catastrophe or merely an

irritant, their approach to dealing with it was the same. Examine your attitude. A positive one will help you see and seize opportunities. They exist in the most miserable of circumstances. A negative attitude on the other hand locks your thinking into lack and despair leading to more of the same. If you get your thinking straight you, not circumstances, will direct your life. Always look for the upside of a down in a situation. It's there for those willing to see it.

Printed in the United States
By Bookmasters